Lawns

An Uncomplicated Guide

Luke Taylor   Marc Kerr

PAVILION

Introduction

These books usually start with a solid introduction about the authors, their credibility, expertise, and why they've decided to put this book together for you, the reader. You'll be glad to know we're no different. Welcome to *Lawns: An Uncomplicated Guide*, where we strip away the confusion and jargon surrounding lawn care and give you straightforward, practical advice you can trust, from professionals with decades of experience.

First of all, allow us to introduce ourselves: we are Marc Kerr and Luke Taylor. Together we founded the lawn care brand So & Mo, after spending a combined thirty years in the industry 'on the tools'. So & Mo is a brand that simplifies the feeding and nutritional side of lawn care by delivering the right feed, applied at the right time, and tailored to the size of our customer's lawn.

For the past few decades, Marc has been building and maintaining some of the world's best sports surfaces, specifically focusing on golf course construction and greens maintenance in the UK, Europe, and the USA. He began his journey as a trained greenkeeper in the North East of England, then moved to America to develop his knowledge, before returning to join one of Europe's most reputable golf course construction firms. Taking the plunge in the early 2000s, Marc set up on his own and has worked his way to being one of the most trusted contractors for the UK golf industry, working on some of the finest surfaces in the country.

Luke comes from the landscaping and gardening side of the industry, and started his career with his own local maintenance company in the North West of England, which grew from cutting lawns to building designed gardens, before he moved on to specialize in the fascinating world of turf and constructing specialist projects, which is where he met Marc.

As a team we went on, not just to build large private lawns, grass tennis courts, and golf greens, but to maintain them to the highest standard year-round.

After a number of years, we started to question why the lawn-care industry felt so complicated to the homeowner, why there was such a vast array of products that didn't perform as well as the ones we used in the professional world and mostly, why there was absolutely no support available – leaving the untrained customer to select the right product, figure out the right time to undertake the correct lawn-care process, and practically work it all out for themselves.

We created this book to help lawn owners like yourself understand and manage your space with confidence. Lawn care doesn't have to be complicated, yet it's often presented as a maze of conflicting advice and technical terms.

In reality, everyone can achieve a healthy, thriving lawn with the right knowledge (us) and a little effort (you).

Through this book, we aim to simplify the essentials of lawn care – whether you're dealing with weeds, improving soil health, or choosing the right tools. We've distilled our years of expertise into easy-to-follow steps and actionable tips, cutting through the noise to give you exactly what you need to know.

So, whether you're starting from scratch or looking to elevate your current lawn game, we're here to guide you through every step of the way. Let's make lawn care uncomplicated, enjoyable, and rewarding. Your lawn deserves it, and so do you.

Grass may seem like a simple plant, but it's one of the most adaptable and essential elements of our environment. From the sprawling lawns in our gardens to the vast fields of wheat and rice that feed the world, grasses belong to the diverse *Poaceae* family. What makes grass unique is its growth habit - unlike trees and shrubs, it grows from the base rather than the tip, allowing it to be mowed and grazed while continuing to thrive. Beneath the surface, an intricate network of roots provides stability and resilience, helping grass plants withstand changing seasons and environmental stresses. Understanding how grass functions at a biological level will reveal why it's such a vital and enduring part of our landscapes.

The Grass Plant

Biology

Grass, although it might seem simple, is a fascinating part of our environment. It belongs to the plant family *Poaceae*, a diverse group that includes wheat, oats, and even bamboo. The type of grass on your lawn, whether it's ryegrass, fescue, or bentgrass (we'll come on to this later) has unique traits that make it tough, bright, and perfect for creating that inviting patch of greenery in your garden.

Grass grows from the base upwards, not from the top down like trees or shrubs. At the bottom of each blade is a growth point known as the crown, which sits just at or below the soil surface. This crown is the plant's control centre, constantly producing new leaves and roots. It is also the reason mowing doesn't harm your lawn; **as long as the crown remains healthy, the grass carries on growing**. Beneath the soil, a dense network of roots works to absorb water and nutrients to help the plant grow.

Most lawn grasses are perennials, meaning they come back year after year. The plants can go dormant during tough conditions, such as prolonged dry spells or freezing winters. During dormancy, the blades may brown or thin out, but the roots stay alive, ready to produce fresh growth as soon as conditions improve.

Grass plants have a clever way of growing and spreading called tillering. From the base of the plant, or the crown as we now know, small shoots known as tillers emerge. These tillers are essentially new stems that grow alongside the original plant, helping the grass to thicken and fill in bare spots naturally.

DID YOU KNOW? Tillering is encouraged by proper mowing, feeding, and watering practices, as a healthy crown produces more tillers, leading to a healthier, more resilient lawn.

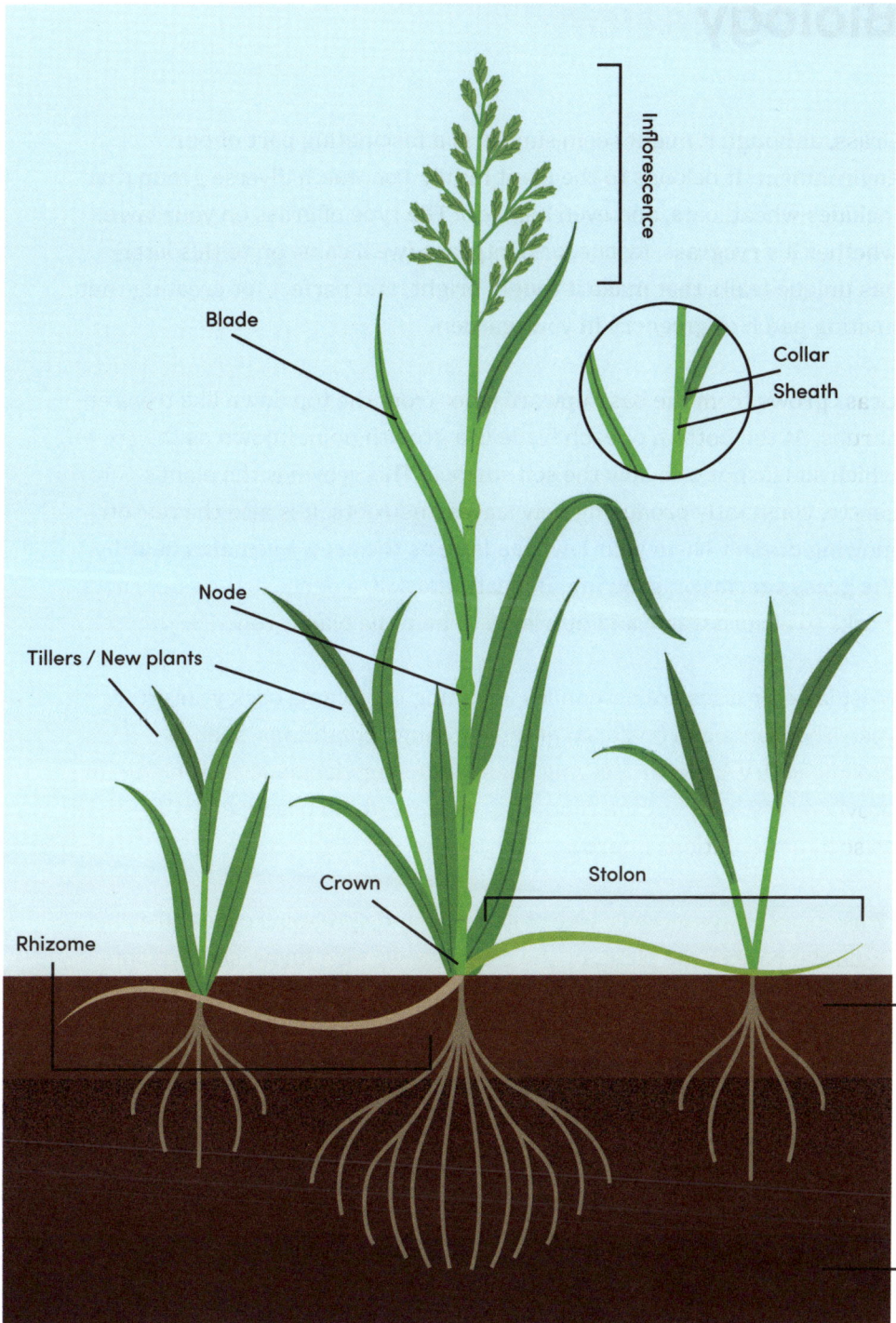

Inflorescence

Blade

Collar

Sheath

Node

Tillers / New plants

Crown

Stolon

Rhizome

Roots

Germination

Germination is the process through which a seed begins to grow into a plant. When the right conditions are met – usually warmth, moisture, and oxygen – the seed absorbs water (a phase known as imbibition) and swells. This triggers the seed's embryo to start growing. The seed then breaks down its stored starches into sugars, fuelling the growth of a tiny root, or radicle, which anchors the seed in the soil. This is followed by the emergence of the shoot, which pushes upwards towards the light. With time, this little sprout develops into a full-grown plant.

The weather plays a crucial role in the germination process of grass seed. It's not just about scattering the seed and hoping for the best. The conditions need to be just right. The length of time it takes for grass seed to germinate can be significantly influenced by the weather. The soil temperature and moisture levels are particularly important. If the soil is too cold or too hot, it can hinder the germination process. Ideally, the optimum soil temperature should be between 10–18°C (50–65°F) for optimal germination, but can be as low as 6°C (43°F). Similarly, if the soil is too dry or overly saturated, this can also affect the seed germination rate. The soil needs to be consistently moist, but not waterlogged. It's a delicate balance that can make or break the success of your lawn.

The nutritional content of your soil also plays an important role in the germination process of grass seed. It's like the fuel that powers the engine of germination. If your soil is lacking in essential macronutrients, the seed germination rate can be negatively impacted, leading to a longer wait for your lush, green lawn. A pre-seed lawn feed can be a game-changer in such cases. By boosting the soil's nutritional content, you will provide the seeds with the necessary macronutrients they need to germinate successfully.

Finally, the depth at which seeds are sown can influence their access to moisture and warmth – two key factors in the germination process. Seeds sown too deep may struggle to reach the necessary moisture, while those too close to the surface may dry out or be at risk from predators. The perfect depth for germination is 6 mm (¼ in) into the soil.

Grass Varieties by Climate

There are many different varieties of the grass plant, and these are split into two main categories, cool-season and warm-season grasses. This distinction is based on the climates the plants thrive in and their active growth periods.

Cool-Season Grasses

These varieties are best suited, as the name suggests, to cooler temperatures and actively grow in the spring and autumn. Staying green through much of the year, they prefer climates with milder summers.

RYEGRASS   Ryegrass is a popular cool-season grass known for its quick germination and durability. Its fine, dark green blades create a lush appearance, making it a favourite for lawns, sports pitches, and golf courses. Ryegrass thrives in cooler climates and is particularly valued for its ability to recover quickly from wear, although it benefits from regular mowing and feeding to stay at its best.

POA ANNUA   *Poa annua*, or annual meadow grass, is a common sight in lawns across the UK. While often considered a weed, its bright green colour and adaptability allow this plant to blend seamlessly into turf. It germinates and grows rapidly in cool, damp conditions, but can become patchy without proper lawn care.

BENTGRASS   Bentgrass is prized for its fine texture and dense growth, making it a top choice for golf greens and bowling lawns. Bentgrass thrives in cool, moist climates and is known for its ability to form a smooth, uniform surface. However, it requires regular care, including close mowing and proper watering, to maintain its immaculate appearance.

KENTUCKY BLUEGRASS

Kentucky bluegrass is renowned for its rich, deep green colour and smooth, dense growth. It spreads through rhizomes, or underground stems, allowing the plant to fill in gaps and recover from damage. Best suited to well-drained, sunny areas, this grass is a favourite for creating picture-perfect lawns, although it benefits most from consistent watering and fertilization.

FESCUE
(below)

Fescue grasses are versatile and hardy, ideal for a wide range of conditions. With varieties like tall fescue and fine fescue, this grass offers drought tolerance and shade adaptability. Fine fescue is especially known for its soft texture and is ideal for low-maintenance conditions, making it perfect for most gardens and ornamental lawns.

Warm-Season grasses

These grasses are built to withstand intense heat and thrive in warmer regions of the world. They will grow most vigorously during hot summer months, but most likely will go dormant and brown when the temperatures drop through winter.

BERMUDA

Bermuda grass is a popular warm-season grass known for its toughness and ability to thrive in hot, dry conditions. It forms a dense, resilient lawn that can handle heavy foot traffic, making it ideal for sports fields and high-use areas. Bermuda grass spreads aggressively through both stolons (above-ground stems) and rhizomes (underground stems), filling in bare spots quickly. It thrives in full sun and requires regular mowing and proper watering to keep it looking its best.

ST AUGUSTINE

St Augustine grass is a lush, coarse-textured, warm-season grass that grows well in humid, coastal areas. Known for its tolerance to shade, it is an excellent choice for lawns with limited sun exposure. It forms a dense, carpet-like lawn, but it does need regular care, including proper watering and occasional fertilization, to stay healthy and vibrant. St Augustine grass is also quite salt-tolerant, making it perfect for coastal regions.

ZOYSIA

Zoysia grass is a slow-growing, dense, warm-season grass that is highly drought-tolerant and heat-resistant. It forms a thick, lush carpet that can withstand both heat and moderate shade, making it a great option for lawns that experience varying sunlight. Zoysia is low maintenance once established, but it can take time to fully fill in, requiring patience during the establishment phase. It is ideal for those looking for a durable, attractive lawn with minimal upkeep.

PASPALUM
(below)

Paspalum grass, especially varieties like seashore paspalum, is well suited to hot climates and coastal regions due to its high salt tolerance. It thrives in a wide range of soil types, including sandy soils, and is highly resistant to drought once established. Paspalum grass has a fine to medium texture and grows well in full sun, making it ideal for lawns and golf courses in warmer climates.

Having built some of the best sport surfaces and private lawns, we've got a good idea of what is required to create the perfect lawn. We can not understate the importance of preparation and getting things right underground, as this will pay dividend on the surface. Whether you're beginning with a blank slate, you're rebuilding a garden, or ripping up an old lawn, in this chapter we are going to cover all the elements of lawn construction and getting it right, from the ground up.

Lawn Construction

Equipment

Before getting stuck in, it's best to make sure you have the right tools for the job. Building a lawn is not a hugely complicated process, and can be done with simple tools, the right materials, and good, solid, hard work. If you're going to be creating a large lawn, then you'll probably want to look at larger machinery, or consult some professionals.

TURF CUTTER
if you're removing an old lawn

WHEELBARROW
for moving material

GOOD SHOVEL
to make light work of filling
your wheelbarrow

GOOD LANDSCAPING OR HAY RAKE
for levelling the soil
(16-18 tooth is a good width)

SOME TURFING BOARDS
for laying, we use 12 mm (½ in)
plywood cut into strips

**HALF-MOON LAWN EDGER
OR A KNIFE (WE GO FOR STEAK)**
to cut the turf rolls to size

RELIABLE SPRINKLER SET-UP
that can reach all corners of the lawn

SPREADER
if you're seeding the lawn

Drainage

If you live in an area that sees a lot of rainfall, then installing drainage before you lay your lawn is an investment that will pay you back for years to come.

The best way to start is by planning where the water will drain, either into an existing drainage system or a new soakaway. Be sure to account for gravity, and begin by installing the drain exit point, then work backwards from there. Beginning at the water's exit from the lawn, you want to have a herringbone system of one main line with angled offshoots no more than 2 m (6½ ft) between each one.

You will want to use a conventional drain with a perforated pipe and 10–20 mm (⅜ - ¾ in) pea gravel. The way to create the drain is to dig a trench into the sub-base roughly 50 cm (20 in) deep, and add a layer of pea gravel into the base. Then lay your perforated pipe on top and hold this down as you fill the rest of the trench with pea gravel, ideally 30 cm (12 in) on top of the pipe to ensure proper hydraulic pull (the natural movement of water through soil caused by suction or capillary action) and to stop silts and fine particles from blocking the drain.

There is another level you can take your drainage system to, called a gravel carpet. After you have installed your herringbone of conventional drains, cover the entire lawn area with another layer of pea gravel, which makes the process of water finding a drain much more effective so it can be taken away from the lawn. A gravel carpet can make the lawn prone to drought, especially during the summer months, so only install one if you are able to make sure there is at least 25 cm (10 in) of material on the top and if you're happy to manage the watering in dry periods of the year.

TOP TIP: If your drains are installed too close to the surface, during the summer months, the soil around them will dry out quickly. This can cause the drainage lines to become visible in the lawn, as the grass over the drains will struggle compared to the surrounding areas. To avoid this, it's important to install drains deep enough so they don't affect the lawn's appearance and performance.

Materials

Getting the right soil for your lawn is one of the most important steps in creating a healthy, long-lasting surface and there are more options than ever before to help you get it right.

Let's start with a favourite from the trade: rootzone. This is a carefully blended, quarried mix of loamy soil and sand that delivers excellent results. The loam provides nutrients and structure for healthy grass growth, while the sand aids in drainage and makes it easier to achieve a smooth, level surface. A 50:50 blend of sand and soil is ideal, although a mix of up to 70:30 (soil:sand) can still give a superb performance, especially where drainage or precision levelling is key. Rootzone is particularly useful in wet or unpredictable weather, as it can be worked and laid without compromising the final result. However, rootzone does come at a higher cost and isn't always readily available, so it may not suit every project.

That said, high-quality topsoils and modern compost-enriched mixes are now giving rootzone a serious run for its money. Some of the latest composts, rich in organic matter and tailored for turf establishment, can provide superior nutritional content and support stronger, more resilient root systems. These materials are especially beneficial when seeding a lawn, as they improve germination and early growth.

If you go the topsoil route, opt for a screened soil with a fine grade (1.5 mm to 5 mm maximum) particle size for good drainage to make spreading and levelling easier. Be sure to schedule work during a dry spell, as wet topsoil can be difficult to manage and hard to rake evenly.

Whichever route you choose, premium rootzone, enriched compost blends, or screened topsoil, you'll want to lay down at least 20 cm (8 in) of good growing medium over your sub-base. More is even better. Deep, nutrient-rich soil gives your lawn room to establish strong roots, which can reach down several feet if given the chance.

Preparation

It is essential to spend a lot of time on this step. We cannot stress enough the importance of preparing your levels correctly, and how noticeable small undulations will be once the top surface for the lawn has been laid – which is also incredibly difficult to rectify later on in the process (see page 104). The most important aspect of preparing and levelling for your lawn is patience.

We use a very simple workflow of rake ... compact ... rake again (you'll discover more about compaction overleaf). Repeat this process until you're happy with the levels, which can either be measured by laser level for complete assurance or simply by eye. You'll be amazed at how close you can get the levels just by sight, confirming the old adage: 'If it looks level, then it probably is.'

When raking your material, you'll want to do this in a number of different directions, and continue to change these as you're raking to distribute the soil evenly around the lower parts of the lawn as you rake the higher areas. The constant back and forth motion with the rake will allow the soil to find an even distribution.

For more extreme lumps and bumps use the back edge of the rake to push material into place. You can also use the back of the rake to smooth out the soil and see the levels more clearly.

Lawn Construction

Compaction

A part of your preparation and the next step of the process is compaction, which again is extremely important in ensuring your levels are maintained once the lawn is laid and starts to support traffic.

To do this, the most effective method is the old 'heel in' technique, which involves using your body weight to compact the soil. Take tiny steps, pushing in with your heel, and cover the entire lawn. As you can imagine this always looks good on a timelapse video!

Once the soil has been compacted throughout, you can start to rake the lawn again, but lightly this time, to knock over the tops of your footprints, and start to improve the levels. You can do this process as many times as necessary until you're happy with the standard of the prep work.

TOP TIP: Save a couple of wheelbarrows of soil, so that if there are any low points when you start to rake, you can tip a wheelbarrow of material into the dip, rather than having to drag in from other points around the lawn.

Method One: Turfing

If you are after a quick lawn transformation, then turf is the one for you. Taking your garden instantly from brown to green, turf means your lawn will be ready for play in just a couple of weeks, so it really does have a lot going for it.

However, not all turf is created equal, and there are a few conditions to consider when selecting the correct turf for your new lawn. First, make sure the turf has been grown with a mixture of cultivars you're happy with for your lawn. Second, check the turf has been in the ground long enough to develop a strong root system and density as lifting turf is very stressful for the plant, so it is quite common for patches to struggle after laying. Third, ensure there are no weeds, moss, or pests coming in with your turf; it's hard enough to keep them out when the lawn has been laid.

How to Lay Your Turf

'So, when it comes to laying, you just slap it down, right?' Well, not quite.

First things first: get some turfing boards ready, as you don't want to stand on all your hard work and perfect preparation. This is rule number one for all lawns: no stepping on the prep. You'll need to lay the turfing boards out on your soil first in a couple of rows, before you have enough turf to move the boards over onto the turf instead. Not only do boards protect your preparation work, this process then helps bed the turf in with the weight of foot traffic.

When rolling out the turf, make sure the leading edge is right up to the previous roll, as moving the turf when laid can stretch and tear it. After rolling out the turf, remember to turn down the last edge with your hands (as you would with a roll of paper), so it beds into the ground and isn't pointing upwards.

TOP TIP: For the best aesthetics, we don't like to sow directly perpendicular to the house, as you'll clearly see the 'drill lines'. It is much better to sow parallel to, or in diagonals from, the house.

Method Two: Seeding

There is something deeply satisfying about growing a lawn from seed. There are a host of benefits to this method: complete control of the mixture you're wanting to sow; limiting the potential for weeds, pests or diseases to be brought into your garden; and usually a much stronger lawn.

The process for seeding a new lawn is straightforward, but there are a couple of points you want to get right. The first is to make sure the spreader you're using is set to the correct setting. Sowing seed is measured by grams per square metre (gsm), and for a new lawn you'll want to sow between 35–50 gsm (3-5 grams per square foot). Anything less than this and your coverage is not going to be dense enough; anything over this is going to be wasteful and can also lead to poor growth due to plants competing for limited resources. We like to set the spreader to half of this amount, at approximately 25 gsm (roughly 2 grams per square foot) and do a 'double pass', which means we sow in two different directions, thereby limiting the risk of missing any areas and giving a more consistent, even finish.

When sowing, go at a nice steady pace, try to walk in straight lines, and on the return don't overlap the previous run. The great thing about seeding a new lawn is that it is very clear where you have been, and once you've finished the whole lawn you will have a clear yellow covering.

Once you have finished spreading the seed it is time to rake it into the soil. Germination is best at 6 mm (¼ in) into the ground so use your landscaping rake and, working in lines across, lightly rake the seed into the prepped soil.

The final step is to give the lawn a good dose of water – don't be shy – and find a way of keeping the birds off the lawn, with a homemade scarecrow!

Growing In: Turf

Watering your new turf correctly is the most important step in helping it establish quickly and healthily.

Begin watering immediately after laying to help the grass recover from being rolled and transported, turf can heat up quickly, especially in warm weather. Initial watering is also critical to prevent the turf from shrinking at the edges, which can leave visible gaps and create opportunities for weeds.

For the first two weeks, water the turf once or twice daily, ensuring the soil beneath stays moist. Pay extra attention to the joints between rolls, as they dry out faster. After two weeks, gradually reduce watering to two to four times per week, adjusting based on weather conditions. This encourages the roots to grow deeper in search of moisture.

From week six onward, once the turf has rooted, watering once a week is typically sufficient, but increase frequency during hot or dry periods for up to six months. A good test is to gently lift a corner of the turf: if the soil underneath feels moist, you're watering correctly. Use a sprinkler to cover each area for around 5–10 minutes per session.

Avoid overwatering. Waterlogged soil can cause the roots to rot and invites weeds and lawn diseases. Your goal is moist, not soggy, soil.

Feeding Your Turf

Around 4–6 weeks after laying, it's a good idea to apply a fertilizer. Most turf is pre-fed in the field before harvesting, but by this point those nutrients will begin to wear off. A balanced lawn feed, ideally with a higher nitrogen content, will help the turf continue to grow strong roots and establish fully in its new environment. Feeding at this stage also encourages healthy green growth and helps the lawn resist stress, weeds, and disease as it matures.

Growing In: Seeding

Establishing a lawn from seed requires consistent moisture and a bit more patience than turf, but with the right care, it will develop into a dense, healthy lawn.

Begin watering immediately after sowing. The goal is to keep the top 1–2 cm of soil consistently moist (not saturated) until the seeds germinate — this typically takes 7–21 days, depending on seed type and conditions.

Water lightly once or twice daily using a fine spray to avoid disturbing the seeds. If the soil dries out, germination may stop, so regular watering is critical in the early stages. Once germination begins and seedlings appear, gradually reduce watering to once every other day, increasing the volume slightly to encourage deeper root growth. By week four, watering 2–3 times per week should be enough, depending on the weather.

After six weeks, once the grass is well-established and has been mowed at least once, transition to a more typical watering schedule: around once per week, or more during dry spells.

Feeding Your Seeded Lawn

To give your lawn the best possible start, you can apply a granular pre-seed fertilizer at the same time as sowing or shortly after. These fertilizers are specially formulated to support seed germination and early root development. Once the new grass has germinated and the lawn has visibly filled in with young plants (usually after 4–6 weeks), it's the ideal time to begin folia feeding. Apply a starter or balanced lawn fertilizer with a good nitrogen content to support early development.

Avoid fertilizing with liquids too early (before germination), as this can waste product because grass plants need to be present to absorb this kind of fertilizer.

Now we're going straight into the non-negotiable aspect of lawn care. As you may have noticed, a lawn grows constantly, and occasionally you're going to need to give it a chop. Mowing is by far the most frequent, basic, and important part of lawn care, which can make or break the quality of the lawn, along with the enjoyment of having one. There are quite a few options to consider when it comes to mowing your lawn, and a lot of that is down to personal preference as to what you're looking to achieve, how you want to use the lawn, and the effort you are prepared to put in. From a 'Keep Off the Grass' ornamental lawn, to a football pitch for the kids, you should choose the mowing setup that is going to suit you.

Mowing

Types of Lawn Mower

The mower is the most important tool in your lawn-care arsenal. Choosing the right mower can be a minefield, from the sheer number of options out there (and from a range of different manufacturers), to understanding what model you need to do the job you want, not to mention considerations of price, quality, size, and storage.

To make selecting your mower more straightforward, the first thing to decide is what type you want to go for, and then all the other factors can be whittled down.

Rotary Mower

The most popular type of lawn mower and suitable for most gardens (and gardeners), the rotary mower is a good, solid, and reliable choice. A rotary mower works by spinning a large single blade horizontally within the drum. The suction created by the spinning blade stands the grass up tall for the blade to chop at the desired height. This suction also vacuums up twigs and other debris from the lawn to give a much cleaner appearance (along with saving you a collection job). Powered by either petrol engine, electricity, or battery, these mowers are perfect for lawns that will be maintained at more than 15 mm (⅔ in), are incredibly robust, and require less maintenance than other types of mower. Although suitable for most ornamental lawns a rotary mower will not produce as fine a cut as a cylinder mower. However, as the blade sits off the ground, rotary mowers cope well with undulations and other imperfections in your lawn, cutting longer grass and handling uneven surfaces far better than a cylinder mower.

☑ PROS
- Hard-wearing and durable
- Large range of cutting heights
- Readily available

☒ CONS
- Wouldn't recommend for lawns to maintained at less than 10 mm (⅜ in)
- Can be heavy when used to cut banks/slopes

Cylinder Mower

A cylinder mower, as the name suggests, is a cylinder of blades that trap the sward of the plant against a piece of metal on the bottom of the mower called the bed knife. When the blade and the bed knife come together, they act like a pair of scissors and cut the individual leaf.

If you are a lawn enthusiast and have an ornamental lawn that you want to cut short, below 10–15 mm (⅜ - ⅔ inch), you will get a better, more consistent finish with a cylinder mower. These mowers are far more sensitive than rotary mowers, but when set up correctly and well maintained, they provide a superior-quality cut, perfect for professionals and very keen gardeners. To get the best results from this mower you will need to have a well-maintained lawn without undulations and imperfections, as cylinder mowers can easy scalp patches of the lawn that are raised.

☑ PROS
- Able to cut very low heights
- 'Fine' cutting appearance
- Creates great stripes in lawns
- Gives a clean cut for good plant health

☒ CONS
- Doesn't cut well over 10 mm (⅜ in)
- Costly to buy and maintain
- Needs to be used twice a week
- Not suitable for undulations

Robotic Mower

This mower is the new kid on the block and is taking the industry by storm. A robotic mower autonomously trims grass using sensors, boundary wires, or GPS to navigate and stay within designated areas. It uses small, sharp blades to cut tiny portions of grass very frequently, which is much healthier for the plant, leaving small clippings as mulch that break down quickly and help to return nutrients to the soil.

Most models operate in random or patterned paths to ensure complete lawn coverage, and many can automatically return to their charging stations when needed. Beyond the convenience, robotic mowers promote consistently healthy grass. As they cut frequently, the lawn is always kept at an optimal height — avoiding stress from sudden cuts and encouraging denser, more resilient growth. Some advanced models even adjust their mowing schedule based on grass growth rates or weather forecasts.

Robotic mowers pair especially well with lawn-care plans that deliver the right nutrition at the right time. While the mower maintains the height and health of the grass, your tailored feed programme will ensure it's growing strongly from the roots up — a powerful, low-maintenance combo for a lush and thriving lawn.

☑ **PROS**
- Hard-wearing and durable
- Consistent cut for plant health
- Effortless, quiet and time-saving

☒ **CONS**
- Set-up can be tricky and confusing
- Not suitable for cuts lower than 20–25 mm (¾-1 in)

Hover Mower

A hover mower is simply a rotary mower that sits on a cushion of air instead of wheels, which means it can handle long grass and uneven surfaces. Just like a rotary mower, a single, central blade underneath does the cutting. A hover mower is predominantly a mulching mower where the grass clippings are chopped up and redistributed back onto the lawn so there is no collection box to empty. Cutting heights usually range from 15–60 mm (⅔–2½ in).

☑ PROS
- Lightweight and easy to handle
- No turning wear (e.g. in wheels)
- Good for a range of heights
- Easy to maintain

☒ CONS
- Wouldn't recommend for lawns to be maintained at less than 10 mm (⅜ in)

Ride-on Mower

Reserved for very large lawns, ride-on mowers may be cylinder or rotary. This type of mower will cut down on your mowing time, but is much more expensive than any of those mentioned previously.

Choosing a ride-on model with a wider cut can make a significant difference to the time taken to mow your lawn, so if you don't have time or the inclination, it may be well worth the modest increase in price.

☑ **PROS**
- Hard-wearing and durable

☒ **CONS**
- Wouldn't recommend for lawns to be maintained at less than 10 mm (⅜ in)

Pedestrian self-propelled models are also a cheaper alternative for large lawns.

Mower Maintenance

Once you've chosen your mower and started putting it to work, it is important to keep an eye on maintenance. Maintenance is key for a two main reasons: protecting an expensive purchase and ensuring the highest longevity, and for keeping the quality of cut high to protect the health of the plant. All mowers are different, and require varying levels of service depending on the cutting style and power system, however these simple maintenance tips will cover most lawn mowers and keep them in good order.

KEEP YOUR BLADES SHARP

Whichever type of mower you have, they all use blades to cut, and it's key to the quality of your lawn that you keep these blades nice and sharp. If the blades start to get blunt, this will tear the sward of the plant rather than provide a clean cut, which then make the plant more susceptible to disease.

KEEP IT CLEAN

Following each mowing, it is good practice to remove any debris and grass cuttings from the underside to avoid clogging, and to avoid causing a bad smell. Having a nice clean drum each time you mow will send the clippings into the basket or mulch in the most effective way.

OIL CHANGE AND AIR FILTERS

Keep an eye on the oil level and remove old or contaminated oil, replacing it with new as needed.

Inspect air filters and replace if they are clogged up or dirty. Air filters are quick and inexpensive to replace so it's worth the effort to replace these annually whatever their state.

SPARK PLUGS Spark plugs are also inexpensive and are an important part of the smooth running of your petrol machine. Replace spark plugs as and when required, usually every third year. This will help the mower to start with ease every time (meaning no more ripping the cord!).

If you prefer, take your mower to a professional on an annual basis and they will cover the checks mentioned for you.

! **For specific maintenance instructions for your mower, always refer to the owner's manual.**

TOP TIP: Use winter as the perfect time to undertake all mower maintenance or book in for a professional service when you don't need to rush the mower back into action.

Cutting Height and Frequency

What height should you mow your lawn at? Well, that's completely up to you. This is not us passing the buck, it's quite simply a personal choice. Your lawn can be maintained at whatever height you'd like it to be; the only thing to consider is what you're looking to use the lawn for, and the time and effort you're willing to put in.

Grass is an incredibly versatile plant. It can be as short as 3 mm (⅛ in) for a golf green, all the way to field height measured in metres (or feet). Does short grass require more time and effort to maintain than a lawn at a taller height? Well absolutely, but that doesn't mean it isn't possible. At the other end of the spectrum, leaving your lawn to grow too long has a negative impact, making the plant weak and very thin at the bottom, and leaving lot of space for weeds and other unwanted plants to become established in those bare areas before you are aware of them, as the long lawn disguises the thin nature.

Here are some ballpark numbers for height you can use as a guide.

• If you're looking for a 'Keep off the Grass'-style ornamental lawn we'd plump for 10–15 mm (⅜-⅔ in); anything lower than that, and you will start to exponentially increase the maintenance required, and not necessarily see any more upside.

• A healthy all-round height that will amaze people at the family barbecue, but still cope with a game of football, would be 15–25 mm (⅔-1 in). This gives the leaf enough length to be hardy, hold good colour, encourage good lateral growth, and not be too exposed to diseases.

CUT LIKE THE PROS: Wimbledon Centre Court - 8 mm (⁵⁄₁₆ in) and cut every day / St Andrews Golf Club greens - 4 mm (⁵⁄₃₂ in) and cut every day / Wembley Stadium - 22 mm (⅞ in) and cut up to three times on match days.

• Do be aware that if you are cutting higher than 25 mm (1 in), then you're inadvertently leaving your lawn weakened and open to attack by all things such as weeds, disease, and pests.

Depending on the height you decide to maintain, you'll probably want to reassess this choice during the winter months by raising the amount a little from your 'growing season' length. This will allow the plant some winter bulk to see it through the testing periods of weather. Changing the cutting height can also be necessary during heatwaves.

For optimum plant health, when mowing you want to be cutting as little off the plant as possible, so throughout the growing season, this means you will need to cut the lawn two to three times a week. Now, if mowing the lawn is your happy place, this will be music to your ears; however, if mowing is a task to be done as little and as quickly as possible, then you'll want to be looking at a minimum of once a week throughout the growing season, but bear in mind the longer you let the lawn grow, the longer it's going to take to cut. You never want to be cutting more than a third of the plant at any one time, as this will cause the plant quite a lot of stress, make the plant weak, and make it vulnerable to disease. In addition, the more you are cutting, the more the plant will want to grow horizontally rather than just vertically, which we refer to as lateral growth, and this then makes your lawn look and feel much thicker.

TOP TIP: If you are wanting to cut your lawn more frequently, you'll need to feed the lawn more frequently as well.

Mowing Techniques

It's not just up and down you know. Here we're going to touch on some of the techniques to watch out for when mowing the lawn.

Changing Direction

While many people think that mowing the lawn in different directions is just about making it look neat and tidy, there are several reasons why it is important to do this.

One of the main reasons is that changing direction helps to reduce soil compaction. Soil compaction can occur when you mow the lawn in the same direction every time. The weight of the lawn mower (and you) can cause the soil to become tightly packed, which makes it difficult for water, air, and nutrients to reach the roots of the grass. This complication can lead to a weak and unhealthy lawn.

Another reason is that mowing in different directions helps to prevent the grass from leaning in one direction. When you mow the lawn in the same direction each time, the grass will start to bend that same way. This can make your lawn look uneven and can make it more difficult to mow in the future. By mowing in different directions, you can help to keep the grass standing upright and looking more uniform.

Finally, changing directions can help to encourage even growth. By mowing in different directions, you can help to encourage consistent growth and keep your lawn looking healthy and green.

Take Note of the Weather

It is best to mow your lawn when the grass is dry. Wet grass can clump, which can cause uneven mowing, and can also clog your lawn mower.

Plan Your Mowing Height

You should also keep in mind the height of your lawn-mower blade. Mowing your lawn too short can damage the grass and expose it to stress from the sun. Ideally, you should mow no more than one-third of the grass height with each mowing. Additionally, keep your lawn-mower blades sharp. Dull blades can tear the grass, which can make it more susceptible to disease.

Cutting After a Long Period Away

We've all been there, living it up on holiday for a fortnight, only to come back to a wild field that's grown in the back garden, meaning your precious days before returning to work are taken up with getting the lawn back under control.

The temptation can be to hack away and chop all the long grass back to the right height, but this will massively stress the plant, which has become used to having long leaves to absorb all the sunlight it needs. You'll want to put the mower on the highest setting to start with, and take the overgrown lawn down over a few days, allowing the plant to acclimatize to its new level. We always like to 'double cut', which means cutting twice on the same setting to give a cleaner, healthier cut to the plant. You'll also start to expose the more hidden part of the leaf, which won't be as colourful as the top, so expect a yellow colour for a few days.

Finally, apply a feed to help the grass to get the nutrients it needs to bounce back from the stress, and replace the overfeeding the lawn got used to while you were away.

Creating Stripes

Striped and patterned lawns can be truly impressive. With a bit of care and the right lawn mower, they are easier to achieve than you might think.

The striped effect is created by pushing the grass in opposite directions in order to influence the way in which sunlight reflects on the blades. The blades that are bent away from the sun will reflect the light, creating bright stripes; while the blades that are bent towards the light will create shadows, making the stripes appear darker.

To get stripes in your lawn, you'll need to mow your lawn in different directions with a lawn mower that has a roller. As the lawn is mown, the roller angles the grass blades in opposite directions, creating the two different lighting effects. The lighter stripe is always the direction pointing away from you and the darker stripe pointing towards you.

However, before you start mowing, you must ensure that your lawn is in good, healthy condition, at the right length, and that you have the necessary tools.

MAKE A PLAN

How you stripe depends on the shape of your garden and the effect you want to achieve. Diagonal stripes can make your garden appear bigger, while more irregular spaces may benefit from wavy lines that follow the contour of the space. Once you've got the technique down, the possibilities are endless.

START WITH A MOWER THAT HAS A ROLLER

The type of mower you own is irrelevant, as long as the machine is equipped with a roller. This is the easiest, most efficient, and most effective way to create stripes in your lawn.

MAKE SURE THE LAWN IS LONG ENOUGH

For the optimum effect, make sure that your lawn has a good length before you stripe. The shorter the blades, the harder it will be to bend the grass in the desired direction.

MAKE SURE THAT THE LAWN IS DRY

Mowing your grass when wet is likely to result in an uneven and damaged lawn. When the grass is dry, the blades stand taller, making it easier to mow evenly. Additionally, wet blades are more likely to tear than cut cleanly, opening the door for fungal diseases to settle in.

REMOVE DEBRIS AND OBSTACLES

Ensure your lawn is free from any bits and bobs like twigs, stones, and toys that might spoil the look and even damage your mower.

How long your stripes last will depend on the type of grass and what you use your lawn for. Longer, more flexible grasses will be easier to lay flat, while shorter and more rigid types of grasses are more likely to spring back and lose their stripe definition.

Striping can be done as often as you mow your lawn. In the warmer months, when grass grows faster, you may want to mow your lawn up to a few times a week. During the colder months, it's likely that you can go as long as five weeks between mowing sessions, as the grass grows slower.

Striping the lawn causes no damage at all; as we have learnt, this process is simply leaning the grasses in different directions, meaning there is no stress or damage done to your lawn when doing this. In fact, lawn striping may be beneficial, as changing the direction of the blades frequently allows for sun to reach all the blades more consistently than if you were to mow in the same direction uniformly and repeatedly.

Boxing or Mulching?

When mowing your lawn, you might wonder whether you should collect the grass clippings or leave them to mulch. Both methods have their advantages, and the right choice depends on your lawn's needs and your personal preference.

Boxing or collecting clippings involves using a mower with a bag or box attachment to gather the cut grass as you mow. This approach is ideal if you're aiming for a clean, polished look. It's especially useful after cutting tall grass or dealing with areas where weeds may be spreading, as collecting clippings prevents weed seeds from being redistributed.

Additionally, bagged clippings can be composted, turning them into nutrient-rich material for your garden. However, collecting clippings also removes valuable nutrients that could naturally return to the soil. It also adds extra work as you'll need to empty the bag frequently and find a way to dispose of the clippings, which can contribute to waste if not composted.

Mulching, on the other hand, involves leaving finely chopped clippings on the lawn to decompose naturally. This method acts as a natural fertilizer, returning essential nutrients like nitrogen to the soil and helping to retain moisture. Mulching saves time and effort, as you won't need to stop mowing to empty a bag or worry about disposal. It's also eco-friendly, keeping organic material on site and reducing waste.

However, mulching may not provide the pristine look that collecting clippings does, and if the grass is wet or too long clippings can clump together, potentially smothering the grass beneath. Mulching is most effective when mowing is done regularly and you keep the grass at an ideal length, so when you mow there isn't much waste.

Ultimately, the decision comes down to your goals and values. If you're seeking a tidy, weed-free appearance or have a composting system in place, collecting clippings might be your best bet. If you prefer a low-maintenance, sustainable approach that boosts your lawn's health, mulching is the better option.

WHAT WOULD WE CHOOSE? The main concern of the domestic lawn is weeds, so to keep those from spreading we would opt for boxing. In our opinion the benefits of mulching such as the increase in nutritional value to the lawn, can be massively out-performed by using a proper feeding programme. Plus, you can chalk up the extra trips to the bin as good cardio.

Now you've got your mowing regime dialled in, there are a few big areas of maintenance that you will need to undertake over the course of the year, with frequency depending on your goals for the lawn and the conditions you're dealing with. We must stress this isn't an exact science but, as with everything in lawn care, little and often is always a great starting point. Generally we'd recommend these processes at least twice a year for best results.

Seasonal Maintenance

Seasonal Maintenance

What is Thatch?

First, we need to introduce you to a naturally occurring part of your lawn. Thatch is a build-up of organic matter that accumulates around the base of the grass plants. It comprises a mix of dead grass roots and stems, clippings, leaves, and other debris that have found their way into your lawn, forming a dense, fibrous layer just above the soil.

Thatch occurs naturally in most lawns, and its effects on the health of your grass depend on how it is managed. A small amount of thatch is normal and quite healthy; it can cushion and protect the crown of the grass and shield the soil from the elements. However when left to build up, thatch can be detrimental to your lawn.

An accumulation of thatch will prevent air, water, and nutrients from reaching the roots of your grass, as well as being the perfect breeding ground for moss and lawn diseases. If left to increase, thatch will act like a sponge, absorbing all the water and drying out the soil. A dry soil will then force the grass to grow roots back into the thatch, making your lawn spongy and irregular.

In ideal conditions, thatch is decomposed by naturally occurring bacteria and fungi which break down the layers, maintaining a healthy balance for your lawn. However, due to natural components in the grass that slow down decomposition, your lawn often grows quicker than the old grasses can be broken down by bacteria. So, over time, excess thatch builds up in your lawn and external intervention is needed to keep your grass healthy.

Now, onto scarification ....

Scarification

Lawn scarification, often referred to as 'scarifying' or 'dethatching', is a crucial part of lawn care. It's a process that involves vertically cutting through the lawn and removing the layer of thatch (which we have just discussed). This process is done using a scarifier, which is a tool equipped with rotating blades that penetrate a few millimetres into the soil. Scraification can also be achieved with a spring rake (and some good, old-fashioned hard work).

The purpose of scarification is not to damage your lawn, but to rejuvenate it. The procedure might seem a bit messy at first, but it's beneficial for your lawn in the long run. Scarification helps with removing moss, thatch, and weeds, making it easier for air, water, and micronutrients to reach the roots of your grass plants.

STEP 1: THATCH-HEAVY ⟶ STEP 2: SCARIFICATION ⟶

This process also helps to aerate your lawn, allowing it to breathe and absorb nutrients more effectively, which aids growth.

In essence, lawn scarification is a vital process in maintaining a healthy, lush garden. It's a bit like giving your lawn a deep cleanse, removing all the unwanted debris and allowing it to breathe and grow better. We can't stress enough the importance of this process, so read on to discover when and how to complete it.

STEP 3: REPEAT THE PROCESS

STEP 4: HEALTHY GROWTH

When to Scarify Your Lawn

Understanding when to scarify your lawn is crucial for maintaining its health and vibrancy. The timing can significantly impact the effectiveness of scarification and the overall condition of your lawn. The best time to scarify largely depends on the condition of your turf and the weather. Generally, spring and early autumn are ideal, as you have warm temperatures for recovery and some rainfall.

For lawns under constant shade, late March through April is the best time to rake. This is when tree crowns are at their thinnest, allowing maximum sunlight for optimal growth. Avoid the wrong time for scarification, such as during the summer months, as the heat and dry conditions slow down grass recovery, leaving your lawn vulnerable and parched. Similarly, in winter the grass goes dormant in the cold, and any raking can expose your soil to harsh weather, leading to frost heave (when the ground swells due to ice) and moss invasion with no growth to repair what you've removed.

Tools Required for Scarifying a Lawn

The size of your lawn is a key factor in this decision. For smaller lawns, a wire rake or manual scarifier might suffice, but for anything over 50 sq. m (538 sq. ft) we would definitely recommend a powered scarifier.

Remember, the scarifier's blades should be sharp and adjustable. This allows you to control the depth of scarification, preventing damage to your lawn. You want to have the blades just touching the soil: any deeper and you'll bring good soil up and make a mess; anything too high and the process won't be effective.

USING A RAKE FOR SCARIFICATION

Scarifying your lawn with a rake is a viable option, especially if you're dealing with a smaller garden. This method, while labour intensive, can be effective in removing thatch and moss. However, it's important to note that using a rake for scarification can be physically demanding. It requires a good deal of effort and can be time-consuming, particularly for larger lawns.

- Before you start, ensure your lawn is free of any debris such as sticks or rocks that could interfere with the process. Mow your lawn to about 2.5 cm (just under 1 in) in height and collect any clippings.

- When scarifying, move the rake in parallel lines, overlapping each pass slightly. After scarifying, collect the debris with the rake and dispose of it.

- Remember, scarifying with a rake is a manual process, and may not be as thorough as using a scarifier. However, it can still be a beneficial method for maintaining the health of your lawn.

A Step-by-Step Guide to Scarifying Your Lawn

Before you start the scarification process, prepare your lawn adequately. Start by mowing your lawn to a height of around 2.5–3 cm (¾–1 ¼ in). This step is essential as it allows the scarifier's blades to reach the soil surface effectively and removes long grass from getting in the way. Next, ensure that your lawn is free from any debris such as sticks, rocks, or large stones. These can interfere with the scarification process and potentially damage your scarifier. Finally, bear in mind that scarification can be a messy process. So, be prepared to clean up the loosened thatch afterwards with a rake or a tool with a grass catcher box.

First, set the depth of the scarifier. This will be determined based on the age of your lawn and the extent of thatch that needs to come out.

As a general rule, the blades of the scarifier should not rip open the ground, but rather lightly skim the soil surface. This means adjusting the blades to penetrate the ground to a depth of 2–3 mm (1/16 in). You can test this depth on a small section of your lawn and readjust if necessary. If your lawn has been neglected for a while, you may need to go deeper.

Use the scarifier as you would the lawn mower, walking up and down, pushing it as you go with the waste spitting out at the back. We would make three to four passes when scarifying in different directions to make sure you cover the majority of the lawn.

TOP TIP: We often see lawns which their owners claim to have scarified but the amount of thatch left is huge, so don't be shy! You'll be surprised how much waste can be produced and if thatch is still coming out when you scarify, keep going.

What to Do after Scarifying

After you're finished, your lawn will look in quite a sorry state, but this is temporary and soon you'll witness a lusher, more vibrant lawn. The first step post-scarification is to remove all the waste. If your scarifier doesn't have a grass-catcher box, use a rake to do this.

If you notice larger bare patches on your lawn, the next thing to do is to overseed. This involves spreading grass seeds over the existing lawn to fill in the bare spots and create a denser, greener lawn.

After that, it's time to nourish your lawn, and give it some energy to recover from the stressful process of scarification. Apply a good-quality fertilizer and, if you want to improve the germination of your grass seed and the levels of your lawn, now would be the time to top-dress.

You should wait until you see new growth appearing before you mow your lawn again. This typically takes about two weeks, depending on the weather and the health of your lawn. Remember, the goal is to allow the grass to recover and grow back stronger. Mowing too soon can hinder this process and cause unnecessary stress to your lawn.

Aeration

When it comes to lawn care, our thoughts are that little and often goes a long way. This rule applies to mowing, watering, and even fertilizing. There are also some lawn-care tasks that, although needed less regularly, are essential to the maintenance of healthy and resilient grass, and one of those is aeration.

Aeration is the process of creating lots of small holes, which act as channels of air all over the lawn, by using either solid tines, which push the soil down, or hollow tines, which bring cores back to the surface.

Aerating your lawn helps break down compacted soil and facilitates the penetration of water, oxygen, and nutrients into the ground, which in turn increases the beneficial microbial environment and strengthens the root system. Additionally, well-aerated lawns perform better under severe conditions of drought and waterlogging.

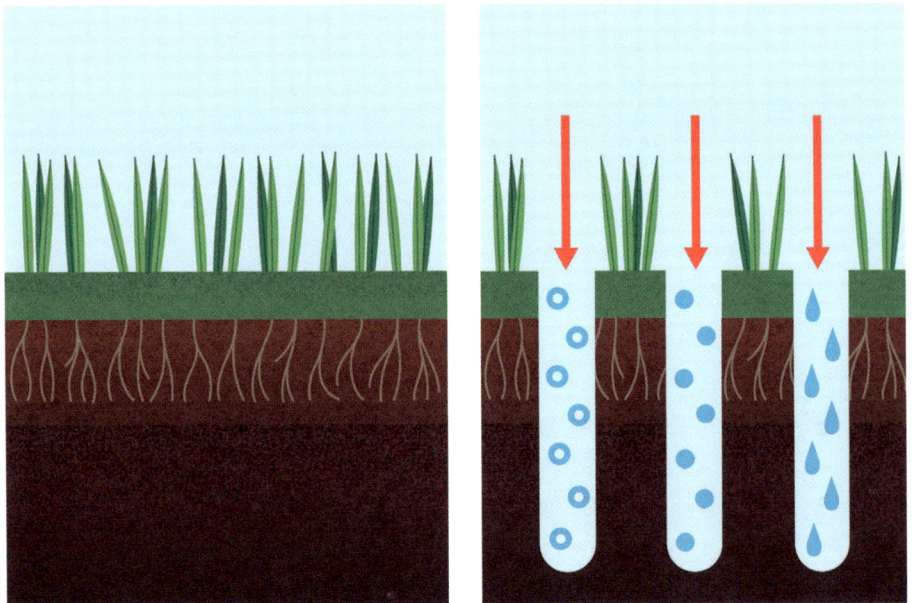

STEP 1: CHOKED AND DENSE LAWN ⟶   **STEP 2: AERATION** ⟶

Bacteria play a vital role in your lawn, helping maintain the health and the efficiency of the root system. Soil naturally contains oxygen and nutrients that support a healthy balance of microbes required for a healthy lawn. However, over time soils can become compacted, and when this happens the natural supply of nutrients, water, and oxygen is reduced — negatively impacting the healthy microbial environment.

We recommend that lawns are aerated once a year as a minimum. As the process is highly beneficial, you can actually aerate as often as necessary. Heavily compacted lawns, areas used as footpaths, and shady areas, require more frequent care due to heavy use, compaction, and a lack of air movement, in which case aeration can be carried out up to six times a year.

→ **STEP 3: HEALTHY GROWTH**

When Should You Aerate Your Lawn?

Just like scarification and other annual tasks, aeration is a fairly stressful procedure for your lawn, and it should be carried out during periods of growth when the grass plants can quickly recover.

For cool-season grasses, like those commonly found in the UK and the northern USA, aeration should be done during early spring or autumn, while warm-season grasses, often found in Australia and southern USA, should be aerated in late spring.

Before getting started, make sure you keep an eye on the weather forecast, and try to match your aeration to a week of good (or warm) weather, as heavy rainfall will wash over the soil and block the channels created during the aeration process, thereby defeating the purpose.

Types of Aeration

A mentioned earlier, there are two types of aeration: solid-tine and hollow-tine.

Solid-tine aeration is when you use solid spikes to punch holes into the lawn. These move the compaction further down the soil profile, ideally below the root system, and to the side to create the space for the plants to grow without having to make any mess or remove soil.

Hollow-tine aeration, also known as coring, uses hollow cylindrical tines punched into the lawn to create holes across your lawn.

DON'T FORGET: Hollow-tine aeration will bring 'cores' of soil back up to be deposited on the surface. They will sit on the grass but can then be tidied up and taken away.

How to Aerate Your Lawn

Depending on the size of your lawn and condition of the soil, aeration can be carried out either by hand or powered aerator. On most occasions, using a garden fork is the simplest method of aeration for small-sized garden lawns, but we'd recommend a machine-powered aerator for any area larger than 50 sq. m (538 sq. ft). For heavily compacted gardens, we recommend using a hollow-tine aerator. These kinds of machines pull cores of soil from the ground to create space for the rest of the soil to move and de-compact. The size and depth of these cores depends on the type of machine used.

Whichever method you choose, there are a few tasks to carry out before and after the process that will ensure that your lawn receives maximum benefit.

PREPARE YOUR LAWN

It is a good idea to mow your lawn a few days in advance: remove any debris and obstacles, and check for underground hazards like ground pipes.

Additionally, if your lawn is in need of scarification, you should do this before you aerate it.

PREPARE YOUR SOIL

Watering your lawn a day in advance, or waiting for the day after a rain shower, will make the process of aerating far easier than trying to break through dry, hard soil.

AERATE BY HAND

There are a number of dedicated tools you can use to aerate your lawn by hand, including spiking shoes, manual spike aerators, and manual core aerators. However in most cases, a garden fork will do the job.

- Insert your garden fork roughly 15 cm (6 in) deep into the soil.

- Push forwards as you remove the fork from the soil. This will help to make the holes slightly bigger, and create further cracks for aeration, as well as allowing you to easily remove the tool from the soil.

- Continue this process, spacing the holes around 13-15 cm (5-6 in), until you cover the whole surface of your lawn.

AERATE BY MACHINE

Powered aerators can be hired from lawn and garden centres and are equipped with either solid or hollow tines. These aerators are ideal for bigger gardens, as they make the whole process easier and less time-consuming. Go over the surface of your lawn in parallel straight lines where possible, just like when you are mowing.

Aerate the perimeter of your lawn last, to ensure that you are not turning over an already aerated area.

Once finished, go over the surface of your lawn and check for any plugs that may still be in their holes, removing them to free the channel and let in air. Let the plugs dry on the surface of your lawn.

Once dry, they can be broken down and evened out with the soil, using a brush, to ensure that all the nutrients return to your lawn.

What to Do After Aeration

To maximize the benefits of aerating, we recommend applying a top dressing to your lawn (see pages 72–75 for more details). This helps improve soil structure by filling the aeration holes, reducing future compaction, and enhancing the soil profile, especially when using a sand-based mix which over time will improve the drainage of the lawn as well.

Post-aeration is also the ideal time to overseed and fertilize, giving new grass seed the best chance to establish (see page 76 for how to do this effectively).

Finally, to make the most of this intensive care process, be sure to maintain a consistent watering and mowing routine throughout the year.

Top-dressing

Top-dressing is the practice of adding a thin layer of dressing mixture to the surface of a lawn. The dressing mixture usually contains a combination of sand, compost, and soil. The primary purpose of top-dressing is to improve the quality of the soil profile, which leads to a healthier lawn. Top-dressing can also help to level out any uneven surfaces in your lawn and to improve drainage.

Over time, the soil in your lawn can become compacted, which can prevent water and nutrients from penetrating the surface. This can lead to poor growth, yellowing, and thinning of the grass. Top-dressing can help to break up compacted soil, allowing water and nutrients to penetrate to the roots of your grass.

How Does It Work?

The idea of top-dressing is to improve the quality of your soil profile, after the lawn has been established. We have already emphasized the importance of preparation during the construction of a lawn, but there are situations where this isn't possible, such as when you've moved into a new house or if the existing ground has settled over time. When you top-dress a lawn you put a lovely thin mixture (one you'd like the lawn to have been built on) into the base of the grass plant, which will then be integrated down into the top of the soil profile. The more you top-dress, the more the profile will develop into one consisting of fine materials, not the low-quality stuff often used by house builders.

TOP TIP: Do not use building sand, grit, or sharp sand, as this will just lock up your lawn and have the opposite effect.

Do You Need to Top-dress Your Lawn?

Whether you need to top-dress your lawn depends on its condition.

If your lawn has poor soil quality, top-dressing can help to improve it. Similarly, if you have an uneven lawn, this process will help to level it. Finally, if your lawn has poor drainage, you can improve water infiltration via implementing top-dressing.

However, not all lawns require top-dressing. If your lawn has good soil quality, is relatively level, and has good drainage, then top-dressing may not be necessary.

HOW TO TOP-DRESS YOUR LAWN

Top-dressing your lawn is not difficult, but it does require some planning and preparation. Here are the steps you need to follow to top dress your lawn:

- Mow your lawn to a shorter length than usual. This will make it easier to spread the soil mixture evenly across your lawn and get it into the base of the plants.

- Choose the right mixture for your lawn. The soil mixture should contain a combination of sand, compost, and soil. We would use a 50:50 ratio of sand and recycled soil.

- Spread the soil mixture evenly across your lawn using a shovel or a specialized top-dressing machine. If you have a larger lawn, we'd first make piles of top dressing spaced evenly and distribute from those.

- After spreading the top dressing, use a lute (pictured), rake or a brush to work it into the base of the grass. This will help to break up any clumps and ensure that the soil mixture is evenly distributed.

- Water your lawn immediately after top-dressing. This will help the soil to settle and avoid damaging the grass.

Overseeding

Overseeding is a crucial part of lawn care that is often overlooked and misunderstood, and the results of which are very beneficial and worth the effort. The grass plants in your lawn are living organisms, and unfortunately this means that, sometimes, they die.

The grass plant is a very hardy one, but is sometimes given too much credit, and people assume it will live forever. This is not actually the case, and, over time as these plants die off, your lawn can become thin and patchy due to foot traffic, weather conditions, and a multitude of other factors. This is why you need to be regularly adding new grass plants to the lawn, in a process called overseeding.

Overseeding helps boost the density of your grass, filling in those bare spots and creating a more uniform appearance. A denser lawn also helps to prevent soil erosion and weed growth, as the fuller grass leaves little room for other plants to take root.

Adding new seed to your lawn can also improve the health of your lawn. Older lawns may have weaker or damaged grass, which can make the plants more susceptible to disease and pests. By adding new seed, you can introduce newer, healthier grass varieties, which are better equipped to withstand environmental stressors.

Lastly, the newer grass varieties you add may require less water and maintenance, making them a more sustainable choice for your lawn.

What to Use for Overseeding

When overseeding, try to use a seed mixture that matches the seed mix with which you've sown the lawn or one of the same variety that the turf was made with. This can often mean a combination of seed types, but as a general rule always try to match the seed with what your lawn consists of already.

When to Overseed the Lawn

The best time to overseed your lawn is either in the spring – March to early May – or early autumn – late August to September. The latter is best as you will have much less competition in terms of weeds coming through at this time of year. However, and this is a big one, you can overseed any time of the year as long as the temperature is about 6°C (43°F) – the minimum germination temperature.

These are also the months where you would be looking to scarify the lawn, and overseeding is so much more effective if you're able to do it post-scarification. The reason for this is that scarifying your lawn actually creates a seed bed with the indentations you make in the profile, and as you are 'planting' the seed at its perfect depth of 6 mm (¼ in), this will dramatically increase germination.

HOW TO OVERSEED YOUR LAWN

- Remove or kill off any weeds or moss. You'll want to do this at least a couple of weeks before overseeding as the products used can hinder germination and kill off seed.

- Mow your lawn as low as possible to allow the seed to get right down into the soil.

- If necessary, scarify or rake any thatch that has built up and remove it. A thick layer of thatch will prevent seeds from germinating and establishing as they won't be able to plant themselves in the soil.

- Relieve any compaction, through aeration (pages 64-70) to create more air and help the seed to get going quickly.

- Evenly distribute the seed over the area you're overseeding at a rate of roughly 15 gsm (roughly 150 gm per sq. ft).

- Lightly rake over the seed once sown to ensure the seed is in contact with soil and can therefore germinate.

- If possible, add a top dressing and cover the seed for great germination results (page 72-75).

- Give the lawn a good soaking of water.

'Growing It In' after Overseeding

The work doesn't stop here, and the most important part of the process is to grow the new seed in, by getting the best germination you can to make your hard work pay off.

You will want to keep the soil and seed moist for a good couple of weeks, and even if you start to see early germination be sure to maintain the moisture, as not all seeds will germinate at the same time. Soil conditions can vary quite severely within your lawn, so don't assume it's going to perform in a uniform way.

The seed will have enough fertilizer within it for the plant to germinate and start to root, but after this point you will want to give the plant as much help as possible. Once you have a good coverage of new leaf it's time to apply a liquid feed (if you haven't put a pre-seed granular fertilizer in the soil already).

Finally, there is the question of when to start mowing, and the answer is probably much sooner than you think! What to avoid when it comes to new grass is leaving it too long before cutting and for the plant to become 'leggy', which means there is too much vertical growth making the lawn look healthy from a distance, but on closer inspection being very sparse and weak. Once you have a high coverage and the sward is strong enough to walk on, we would start a cut taking off very, very small amounts to start with, so that this encourages the plant to search for nutrients and grow laterally as well as vertically, which produces a stronger, denser lawn.

Verti-cutting

Verti-cutting is an important practice that many people overlook, yet it plays a vital role in maintaining a healthy, high-performing lawn. While it might sound a little unconventional, verti-cutting is a highly effective method for improving soil aeration and promoting stronger grass growth.

The process uses a machine equipped with vertically oriented blades that slice down into the soil surface. Rather than just clearing thatch, verti-cutting actually opens up the soil profile, creating small channels that allow water, oxygen, and nutrients to penetrate deeper into the root zone. This improved movement of essential elements helps to support a stronger and more resilient lawn.

While thatch removal can still occur as a side benefit, the primary goal of verti-cutting is to break up compacted soil and create the right conditions for vigorous grass growth. By cutting through the upper soil layer, verti-cutting stimulates new shoots to develop, resulting in a denser, healthier lawn over time.

Regular verti-cutting also enhances the appearance of your lawn, encouraging even growth and reducing the risk of dry patches or weak spots. It's a powerful tool to incorporate into your ongoing lawn-care programme, especially if you're aiming for a lush, professional-looking finish.

Moss Control

Moss is a common issue in lawns. When conditions are dark and damp, you may notice moss appearing around your garden, especially in the autumn and winter months in the UK.

Moss is a type of plant, in a group known as Bryophytes. These are spore-producing, non-vascular plants, meaning that they lack a number of characteristics we are used to seeing in plants, such as leaves, branches, and roots. Mosses grow in many different environments, and are highly adaptable, meaning that they can easily take hold anywhere with the right conditions – including your lawn!

Is It Bad to Have Moss in the Lawn?

Yes, get it out of there! Moss can grow in almost any type of soil and, if left to spread, it can quickly overtake your grass, forming dense, irregular, spongy mats. Not only does moss ruin the aesthetic appearance of your lawn, but it also negatively impacts the health of your grass.

Moss suffocates the grass by competing for growing space and prevents essential water and nutrients from reaching the grass roots by absorbing them on the surface. In addition, during the drier months, moss will die, leaving behind unsightly bald patches on your lawn.

Why Do I Have Moss in My Lawn?

The main cause of a mossy lawn is excess water, as moss is 90 per cent water and thrives in moist environments. Water excess can be due to poor drainage, poor soil quality or high clay content, weak grass roots, and prolonged wet-weather periods. Other issues that can encourage moss to take hold are shady spots, poor air circulation, poor lawn-care and mowing practices, and underlying health conditions that weaken your lawn.

How to Get Rid of Moss in Your Lawn:

Moss can be controlled through a good lawn-care routine alone.
A summary of these steps is below.

SCARIFYING

Scarification is the process of removing thatch, a layer of organic matter
that accumulates at the base of your lawn over time. Thatch stores
moisture and creates an ideal environment for moss to develop. By
regularly scarifying your lawn you'll remove thatch and moss, and improve
aeration and drainage, helping to prevent future issues.

Scarification comes with the additional benefit of creating stress on the
moss plant, which prevents its development as moss does not like to be
disturbed. (See pages 58–63 for more information on scarifying.)

IMPROVING SOIL DRAINAGE

Another effective way of dealing with moss naturally is to improve the
drainage of your lawn so that no excess water is held in the top layer, as
this is where the moss grows. Aerating your soil is a good way to ensure
that water and air can move at the root level, making your lawn healthy
and preventing the surface from becoming waterlogged. (See pages 64–71
for more information on aeration.)

ENCOURAGING GROWTH

When moss spores reach your lawn, the moss plant has to compete with
your grass for space, water, and nutrients. A good strategy for fighting and
preventing moss growth is to promote the health and growth of the grass.

Make sure that you mow your lawn regularly, and maintain a reasonable
length, as a short lawn is more susceptible to moss growth. You can also
encourage healthy lawn growth by ensuring that your grass is properly
nourished by using liquid lawn feed, for example.

USING IRON SULPHATE

Good lawn-care processes, combined with a good feeding programme that includes iron sulphate, can prevent and stunt the growth of moss.

In severe cases, a higher concentration of iron sulphate can be used in the form of a moss treatment. Iron sulphate stunts the growth of the moss to allow for easy removal through good scarification or verti-cutting processes (see pages 58–63 and 81). However, when applied at a high rate, iron sulphate can blacken the moss. So, do take into account that by using the technique, the look of your garden may get worse before it gets better.

How to Prevent Moss

There are over 12,000 species of moss and over 700 of those are present in the UK alone, so the chances are that moss spores of some species are eventually going to reach your grass. To prevent moss taking over, it is important to keep your lawn in good health and maintain a good lawn-management routine, including regular scarification and aeration.

Reconsider your mowing regime, making sure that you mow regularly and don't cut your lawn too short. Similarly, use a good-quality fertilizer programme to encourage vigorous grass growth. Other ways to keep moss at bay are to ensure more light, improve drainage, and keep traffic on the lawn, as moss does not do well under stress.

Will the Grass Grow Back after Moss Removal?

Once the moss has been removed, the space will be free for the healthy grasses to grow into. Regrowth can be encouraged with a good feeding programme. However, if the moss problem has been quite severe, it is best to overseed, as large bare areas leave the soil prone to new problems, such as weeds. The good news is that re-seeding is the perfect opportunity to create a dense lawn of grasses that will stay healthy and resilient.

Now it's time to delve into the world of feeding, NPKs, and photosynthesis. This is a little heavier on the science side, but is extremely important to understand, if you want to get the most from your lawn. As we've said before, the grass plant is a living organism and, just like us, it needs food. Now, the good news is that three meals a day aren't required, and feeding a lawn is a very simple process that is often feared and over-complicated, because people don't quite understand what fertilizer actually is. Understanding the benefits and requirements of feeding the lawn will take you to the next level of lawn care, and the results will really show.

Nutrition and Feeding

How the Grass Plant Makes Energy

Grass is one of the most common plants on Earth, and it is a crucial component of a number of ecosystems. The grass plant is a source of food for many animals and also releases oxygen into the atmosphere, which we breathe.

Grass, like all plants, is an autotroph, meaning it is able to make its own food from inorganic substances. The primary source of energy for the grass plant is photosynthesis, a process that converts light energy from the sun into chemical energy that the plant can use for growth and other processes. During photosynthesis, the chlorophyll in grass leaves captures the energy from sunlight, and uses it to convert carbon dioxide and water into glucose and oxygen. The glucose is then stored in the plant's cells and used as a source of energy.

While photosynthesis is the primary source of energy for the grass plant, it is not the only one. Grass also absorbs nutrients and minerals from the soil through its roots. These nutrients, such as nitrogen, phosphorus, and potassium, are essential for the plant's growth and development.

The grass plant also relies on cellular respiration to produce energy. During cellular respiration, the plant breaks down glucose to release energy for cellular processes.

The Nutrients It Needs and Why

Maintaining a healthy lawn requires a balanced diet of nutrients. Fertilizer is a product, either natural or synthetic, designed to provide extra essential nutrients to the grass plant. Fertilizer typically contains nitrogen, phosphorus, and potassium (NPK), which are essential for grass growth and development. Supplying these nutrients through fertilizer enhances the plant's ability to grow vigorously, develop strong roots, and maintain overall health, rather than forcing it to rely on the limited resources naturally available in the soil. In the same way that we can't perform our best if we're hungry, the same goes for the grass plant.

Below is a list of macronutrients, and a selection of micronutrients, and how they impact the grass plant.

MACRONUTRIENTS

Fertilizer contains macronutrients—nitrogen, phosphorus, and potassium—that are essential for strong growth, root development, and overall plant health.

Nitrogen (N) is used by the plant to produce strong, healthy leaf growth while also encouraging the plant to grow more rapidly and spread, increasing overall density and coverage.

Phosphorus (P) is used to help the plant withstand stress and disease by strengthening the root system; help to support the formation of starches, oils, and sugars; and aid the transformation of sunlight into energy.

Potassium (K) assists with photosynthesis, which leads to growth and vigour, helping the plants to resist disease by keeping metabolic functions running smoothly.

MICRONUTRIENTS

Each fertilizer will also contain some micronutrients. Micronutrients are nutrients that plants need in very small amounts, but they are essential for healthy growth and development.

Iron (Fe) Needed for chlorophyll production. Iron deficiency causes yellowing of the leaves.

Boron (B) Necessary for calcium to perform its functions in the plant. The symptoms of boron deficiency are poor development of the growing tip of the plant.

Copper (Cu) is required for root formation. Deficiency is rare but can occur in sandy, peaty, and chalky soils, which often have high pH levels. A high pH means the soil is more alkaline, typically above 7 on the pH scale, which can limit the availability of copper to plants.

Manganese (Mn) is a micronutrient that helps with photosynthesis and enzyme activity in plants. Manganese deficiency is often caused by over-liming, and is most often found on peaty and sandy soils with a high pH. Symptoms are similar to iron deficiency.

Molybdenum (Mo) enables the fixation of nitrogen but is only required in minute quantities. Deficiency symptoms are similar to nitrogen deficiency (leaf edges may also die).

Zinc (Zn) The effect of zinc deficiency is to hinder the plant's production of chlorophyll. Leaves will show a yellowing while the leaf veins remain green.

Analysing Fertilizer

The properties, strength, and characteristics of a fertilizer are displayed as three numbers separated by a hyphen, such as '17-2-5'. These numbers represent the fertilizer's content of nitrogen (N), phosphorus (as phosphate, P_2O_5), and potassium (as potash, K_2CO_3) — the three primary macronutrients required by every plant.

The three numbers in the fertilizer formulation indicate the percentage by weight of each nutrient in the product. However, it is important to understand that a higher number (i.e. amount) isn't always better; a balanced and seasonally appropriate feeding plan ensures the plant receives nutrients in the amounts it can fully utilize for optimal health and growth.

Following the NPK numbers, you may see additional ingredients listed, such as 'TE' for trace elements (minor nutrients needed in small amounts) and 'Fe' for iron. Nutrients present at less than one per cent are not always required to appear in the guaranteed analysis, so you may need to look more closely at the label or product description to understand the full nutrient profile.

How Fertilizer Is Made

As mentioned above, traditional fertilizer comprises three main chemical elements: nitrogen, phosphorus, and potassium (NPK). Each of these macronutrients are mined differently and, in the interest of keeping this 'an uncomplicated guide', here is an brief overview, for those interested, of how each one is made.

NITROGEN (N)
To make nitrogen available to plants, it must be transformed from its natural atmospheric gas form into a usable compound. This is done using the Haber process,

which reacts nitrogen gas (N_2) from the air with hydrogen gas (H_2) in the presence of an iron catalyst to produce ammonia (NH_3). Ammonia can then be used directly or further processed into solid fertilizers like urea or ammonium nitrate. This process is extremely energy-intensive and is responsible for around three per cent of global annual carbon emissions..

PHOSPHORUS (P)

Phosphorus used in fertilizers is produced from mined ores. Phosphate rock is treated with sulphuric acid to produce phosphoric acid (H_3PO_4), which can then be mixed with ammonia and other raw materials in fertilizer.

POTASSIUM (K)

Most potassium used in fertilizer production is taken from natural deposits of potassium chloride (KCl). The mined material is crushed and purified by the removal of rock particles and salt. Deposits of potassium sulphate (K_2SO_4) and potassium nitrate (KNO_3) are rarer, but when used, are treated in a similar way. Deposits of potassium chloride are also reclaimed from concentrated salts in areas like the Dead Sea in the Middle East.

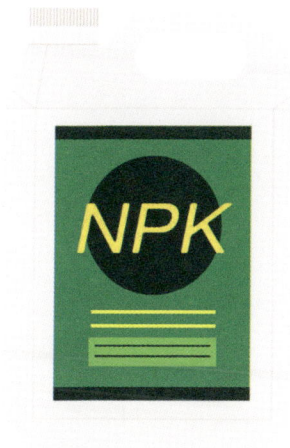

Types of Fertilizer

Fertilizer is applied in two forms: liquid and granular. They both feed the plant, but they go about it in different ways, and therefore have their own benefits and drawbacks.

Liquid Fertilizer

Liquids can come in a ready-to-use or concentrated form to be diluted in water and these can be applied directly onto the lawn to be absorbed by the leaf of the plant. This is known as foliar feeding. The benefits of a liquid feed are listed opposite.

SPEED	As the feed is applied directly onto the leaves, the plants can get going straight away with absorbing the nutrients and sending them round the plant body.
COST	Liquid fertilizers are much more cost-effective to manufacture, so they usually have a lower price point than granular feeds.
PRECISION	It is much easier to be precise with each application in terms of mixing and using every last drop, but it also provides full control of distribution with the sprayer.
STORAGE	With concentrates in particular, you are able to cover a large area with a small volume of packaging, so the product is easy to transport and easy to store.
EFFICACY	They do a really good job (if you get the right stuff), and there is no fall-off in performance.
ERROR	It is almost impossible to get application rates wrong and harm the lawn, so are brilliant for people just getting into lawn care and feeding.
EASY APPLICATION	Can be easily sprayed using various types of garden sprayers, making for a more convenient application process.
PETS AND KIDS	Can typically be a little safer around children and pets due to being diluted before applying, and also being absorbed into the plant straightaway.

Granular Fertilizer

Granular feeds come in a solid, pellet form, and are spread on the lawn to break down in the soil and be absorbed by the plant's roots. The benefits of a granular fertilizer are listed below.

SPEED	A number of granular feeds can start to break down in the soil quite quickly so the plant can absorb the nutrients and put the feed to good use.
STRENGTH	Granular feeds contain a good dose of fertilizer and can be really impactful when it comes to response.
LONGEVITY	Slow-release is a big factor with granular fertilizers, which means they break down over time in the soil, constantly releasing nutrients and lasting up to three months.
AREA	For larger lawn sizes, using a granular fertilizer can be a much more efficient way of feeding the lawn as you're able to broadcast 3 m (10 ft) wide and walk at a fast pace.
DOSAGE	It is easy to measure and apply exactly the right amount of feed for your lawn's size and needs – avoiding overfeeding or nutrient leaching.

Wetting Agents and Surfactants

Wetting agents are, as the name suggests, designed to help to manage water in the plant and are incredibly beneficial during the summer months when rainfall decreases, long periods of heat are common, and the plants start to develop heat stress.

Surfactants, also known as surface-active agents or wetting agents, are substances that reduce the surface tension between two liquids. They are commonly used in a wide range of industries, including household products and pharmaceuticals. By reducing the surface tension between your liquid feed and the water in the plant, surfactant compounds help the feed to stick to the plant rather than roll off it, and allow nutrients and water to penetrate the lawn structure more evenly and efficiently.

Surfactants are available in both liquid and granular form. Here is a list of why you should be looking to include them in your lawn-care plan:

- To improve the uptake of nutrients and other products in the plant.

- For wetting, spreading the feed, penetrating and re-wetting.

- To manage water issues on the plant.

- To guard against plant stress.

- They are safe for beneficial microbes.

- They help to prevent dried-out areas.

- To aid a quick bounce-back after stressful periods.

The Importance of Water

Water is essential for the nutrition and overall health of grass plants, serving as the medium through which nutrients are absorbed and transported, similarly to how we use it in the human body. Water dissolves nutrients in the soil, allowing grass roots to take up essential elements like nitrogen, phosphorus, and potassium. Once inside the plant, water moves these nutrients to different tissues, fuelling growth and cellular processes.

Beyond nutrition, water is critical for photosynthesis. It also helps maintain the plant's structure, keeping cells turgid and their blades upright. Without adequate water, nutrient uptake is impaired, growth slows, and the grass becomes more susceptible to stress, diseases, and browning.

There can be quite a difference, however, between the use of tap water and rainwater. One of the most significant advantages of rainwater is that it is entirely natural and chemical-free. Unlike tap water, which may contain chemicals such as chlorine and fluoride, rainwater is free of contaminants. Another reason why rainwater is better than tap water for watering your lawn is that it is more effective, containing more nutritional value and tends to soak deeper into the soil, reaching the roots of the grass. You can invest in a water butt to collect your rainwater as a sustainable and cost-effective way to make sure you have a healthy supply.

Additionally, tap water is often hard water, meaning it contains dissolved minerals like calcium and magnesium. This can increase soil alkalinity (raise the pH), making it harder for grass to absorb certain nutrients compared to rainwater, which is naturally soft and more balanced for plants.

We all tend to use the lawn in a similar way, therefore there are common issues that we're all going to face as lawn owners. The good news is none of these problems are anything to panic about and, with the right approach, they can all be fixed. Whether it's pets, bare patches, the weather or discoloration, these issues are a natural part of lawn care and can be resolved with simple, effective treatments. Understanding what causes these problems and knowing the best way to tackle them will keep your lawn looking lush and healthy all year round. In this chapter, we'll go through the most common lawn challenges, why they happen, and the practical steps you can take to restore your grass to its best condition.

Common Problems

Dogs and the Lawn

From digging holes to leaving brown spots, dogs can cause a lot of damage. Luckily, there are several ways to repair your lawn and prevent future damage. Below, we discuss three methods for repairing dog-damaged areas on your lawn.

Re-seeding is a common method for repairing dog-damaged areas. To do this, you will need to start by removing any dead grass and debris from the area. Once the area is cleared, loosen the soil with a rake and add a layer of top dressing. Then, sprinkle grass seed over the area and lightly cover it with more topsoil. Be sure to water the area regularly and keep it moist until the new grass begins to grow. This method is effective for small areas of damage and can be done over a weekend.

Turfing is another method that involves removing the damaged grass and soil and replacing it with a patch of turf. To do this, start by cutting out the damaged area with a spade or turf cutter. Then, level the soil and lay the new turf in place. Be sure to water the area regularly and keep it moist until the new turf takes hold. This method is more expensive than re-seeding, but is effective for larger areas of damage.

Prevention is the best way to avoid dog damage altogether. One way to prevent damage is to train your dog to use a specific area of the garden for bathroom breaks. You can also create a designated play area for your dog, to reduce the chances of them digging holes, or trampling the grass. Also consider adding barriers or fencing around areas of the garden that you want to protect.

Repairing dog-damaged areas on a lawn can be frustrating, but it is possible. By using methods like re-seeding and turfing, you can restore your lawn to its former glory. Additionally, by implementing prevention methods, you can reduce the chances of future damage. With a little effort and patience, your lawn can be a beautiful and dog-friendly space for both you and your furry friends to enjoy.

Undulations and Levels

A bumpy lawn is something that we don't like to think about, and many of us would like our back gardens to be as immaculate as the greens of Wentworth Golf Club or the Centre Court at Wimbledon. Unfortunately, with the inconsistency and lack of control over the soil composition, as well as the regular usage and traffic our own lawns are subject to, perfection isn't the case for most lawns, and it is inevitable that undulations will start to appear.

Of course, we wouldn't be telling you this if we didn't have a plan to fix it. However, we must stress that once the turf is laid and the lawn is established, there is only so much rectifying of the levels that you can do.

When the problem is severe, it might require lifting the surface, re-grading the levels underneath, and either re-turfing, re-seeding, or laying the lawn back down. If you're able to use a turf cutter, make sure you are quite gentle. There is no reason why you can't lift the surface, place it to one side, re-grade and level the lawn, and simply put the turf back – just take care and follow all of our hints and tips, on pages 30–31.

If the levels aren't too bad, but they're not perfect and you'd like to see some improvement, the best way to start levelling out the lawn will be through the process of dressing. Using top dressing specifically, and a lute (see pages 74–5) or the back of a rake, you'll be able to inject material into the low spots of the lawn. The reason it is important to use a top dressing or a very sandy product is because this is will be absorbed by the grass plant and moved into the top of the profile, thereby raising the lawn. If you use too much of a dense material, it like a topsoil material will simply sit on top of the grass and kill it off, having the quite opposite desired effect of what you're trying to achieve.

Waterlogging and Puddles

If you live in a rainy climate this is certainly an issue you may encounter. Especially with the volume of rainfall increasing through certain times of the winter (and spring and autumn depending on where you are in the world), it can be hard for your lawn to process this rainfall and move it down through the profile, especially if you don't have a build-up of sandy soil. Depending on the severity of the problem, there are steps at each level you can take to rectify the situation.

Make sure the grass is well fed and healthy, as the longer the root system is, the more water the lawn can absorb on its own.

- Ensure there is no moss in the lawn, as this acts like a giant sponge (see pages 82–84 for more on moss control).

- Reduce the compaction of the lawn and try to introduce more sand into the profile by top-dressing it with a dried sand (see pages 64–71 and 72–75 for more on aeration and top-dressing).

If these steps don't solve the problem to an extent with which you're happy, it might be time to add some drains (see pages 22–23).

Heat Stress

Just like when you've spent too long on the sun lounger in summer without drinking enough water, the grass plant can also develop severe dehydration, which is known as heat stress. The early signs that this is affecting the lawn is the browning of the leaf as it starts to wilt away. This is the plant's first stage of self-protection as it begins to put all of its resources and energy into its root system to stay alive.

A healthy plant that has been regularly fed and well maintained will bounce back incredibly quickly from heat stress. Once the temperatures drop back, you will be able to introduce some water into the lawn, and apply another feed.

To prevent heat stress in the first place, you will need to undertake quite a regimented watering programme to ensure the lawn doesn't dry out and start to wilt. This might be twice a day, depending on the weather conditions and, even then, there is no guarantee that the lawn won't suffer in some way.

Another great prevention technique is to make sure the lawn has been regularly fed with a feed containing a wetting agent or surfactant. This will protect your lawn from drought, therefore reducing the impact of heat stress (see page 98 for more on wetting agents and surfactants). Additionally, a wetting agent will also help the lawn to bounce back much quicker if it does feel the effects of a hot summer.

Oil and Petrol Spills

These are unfortunately quite common in lawn care, often caused by leaky machinery or refuelling accidents. These substances are highly toxic to grass and soil organisms, and even a small amount can quickly kill patches of lawn, leaving unsightly dead spots. The hydrocarbons in oil and petrol block air and water from reaching the roots, locking up the surface, and damaging both the turf and the living soil beneath it.

If a spill happens, acting quickly can make a big difference. Begin by containing the spill with absorbent material like sand, sawdust, or cat litter. Avoid watering the area right away, as this can push contaminants deeper into the soil.

Once the bulk of the liquid has been absorbed, carefully remove the top 5–8 cm (2–3 in) of contaminated soil and dead grass. After the cleanup, gently flush the area with water (for petrol contamination only) to dilute any remaining residue –but only after waiting at least 24 hours.

Follow this by adding fresh material to help to restore microbial life then, finally, re-seed or re-turf the area.

To prevent future spills, always refuel garden equipment away from the lawn and regularly check for leaks. Storing fuel securely and handling it carefully will save you time, effort, and patches of dead grass!

Yellowing in Colour

Whether this occurs just after a winter period or if you've cut the lawn after being away for a few weeks, the lawn can really lose its colour and start to look yellow. This is absolutely nothing to worry about, and quite simply means the chlorophyll of the leaf hasn't had enough sunlight and photosynthesis to green it up. It could also mean the plant is hungry and lacking in nutrients, so it's nothing a good dose of feed and a few days in the sunshine won't fix. Feed the lawn with a fertilizer that is high in nitrogen or contains some iron. These are the two nutrients that are going to boost the chlorophyll in the leaf and improve the colour of your lawn.

Sometimes it's a little bit harder to determine whether the yellowing leaves belong to healthy plants that just need a boost, or if those plants have died off completely. If the plants are still healthy, feeding the lawn will encourage lateral and new growth, helping these stronger grasses spread out and fill in bare patches quickly. However, if the plants have died, you'll need to take extra steps to repair the lawn. First, remove dead grass through scarification (see pages 58–63), then introduce new plants and growth through overseeding (see pages 76–80). Feeding the healthy existing plants will also support this recovery process by promoting dense, vigorous growth to cover the gaps.

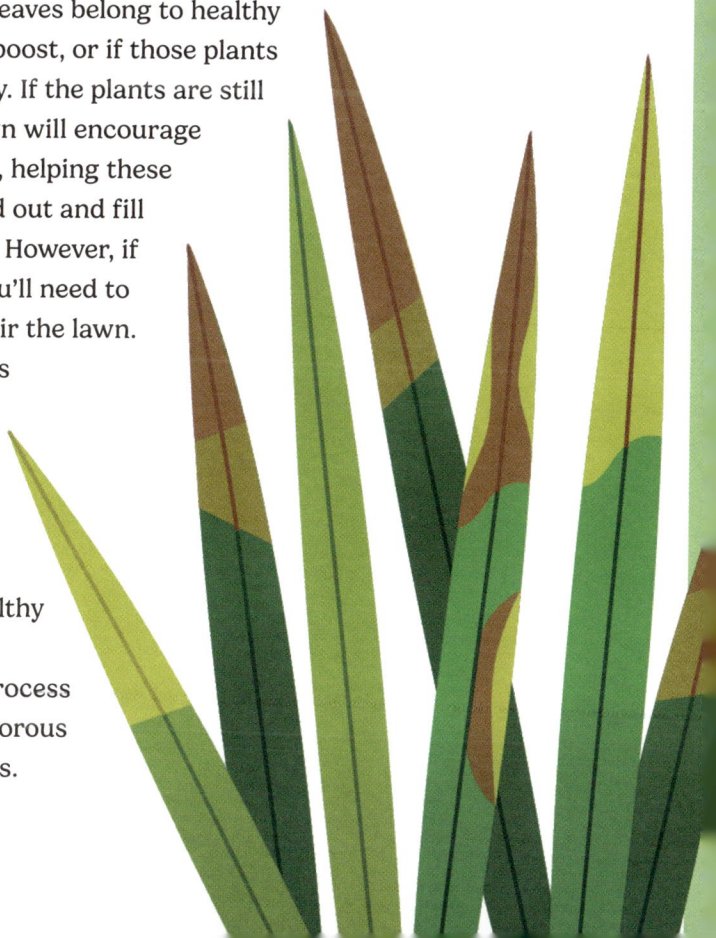

Worn-out Areas

A well-used lawn is a sign of enjoyment – whether it's from a summer of garden parties, kids playing football, or a paddling pool sitting in the same spot for weeks. Unfortunately heavy use can take its toll, leaving behind patchy, compacted, or completely bare areas. The good news? Grass is incredibly resilient and, with the right approach, even the most worn-out sections can be revived. Whether you're dealing with a completely bald patch or just a tired-looking area, the key is to repair, rejuvenate, and rebalance the lawn so it blends seamlessly with the rest. Here's how to bring those worn-out spots back to life.

Completely Bare Areas

We've all been there: the kids are using the lawn like Wembley Stadium and after a few weeks there is a large oval circle in front of the goal (an all-too-common sight on football pitches during the 1990s).

The wear has clearly been too much for that area of lawn, so the fix is to introduce new plants and new growth. There will also usually be heavy compaction in that area and you'll want to break this up to allow the area to thrive again. This is the first thing to deal with. Simply use a garden fork to punch holes in the area and give the soil air to breathe. The next step will be to make sure the levels match the rest of the lawn, so you might need to put down a few bags of material such as rootzone or fine soil, and then use your body weight (see 'heel in' technique, page 29) to compact this down and then rake level. Finally, either finish the job with turf or seed, and follow the same steps we described for constructing a lawn (see pages 18–35).

Check out overleaf for how to salvage worn-out areas that still have some grass.

Solutions

What to do if there's still some grass available

If your lawn has been the home to a paddling pool over the summer, and you've been left with an area that's looking extremely worse for wear but still has good coverage of grass, it's time to give it a revival and bring it back in line with the rest of the lawn.

1. It is likely the grass will be flat and pressed against the ground so the first thing to do would be to lift this back up with a rake or a brush.

2. Then get to work by giving the lawn a cut. This will help to stand the plant up further, cut it to the right height to match the rest of the lawn, and start to encourage it to grow again.

3. The final step would be to give the lawn a feed. You will need to feed the entire lawn rather than just the worn area, as you don't want to start creating a nutrient divide and any noticeable differences in the sections once the grass comes back to full fitness.

Animal Damage

The number of different types of wildlife we have roaming through our gardens can be extremely special to observe – apart from when they are causing damage to your lawn!

We must stress that most animals will not cause damage to the lawn, unless there is a reason for them to do so, which probably means there is an underlying issue. This might be the presence of grubs which animals such as foxes, rabbits, and moles have a tendency to dig for, although the most obvious sign of grubs is the presence of bird damage. (Check out pages 152–3 and 156–7 for advice on how to remove grubs).

The first stage of fixing any animal damage is to determine whether or not grubs are present. If you're able to remove the grub problem, future damage will be prevented.

Mushrooms

Mushrooms sprouting in your lawn can be a puzzling sight. While they indicate a healthy soil rich in organic matter, they can also be a sign of underlying issues. Mushrooms love to grow in soil that is rich in organic matter as they are a type of fungus, and fungi are nature's decomposers. They break down organic material, like dead leaves and grass clippings, into nutrients that can be used by other plants.

Mushrooms are just the visible part of a much larger fungal network beneath the soil. So even if you remove the mushrooms, the fungi will still be there, ready to sprout new mushrooms when conditions are right.

Although mushrooms are a sign of a healthy, nutrient-rich soil, some species can pose a real hazard in lawns. For instance, certain types of lawn mushrooms are poisonous, which can be a serious concern if you have curious pets or little ones who love to explore the garden.

Mushrooms popping up in your lawn can also be a sign of underlying issues with water and drainage. When your lawn has poor drainage, it creates a wet environment that mushrooms love. The excess water combined with organic matter like decaying leaves or grass clippings, provides the perfect food source for fungi, leading to the growth of mushrooms. It's not just about the water on the surface, but also about the moisture retained in the soil.

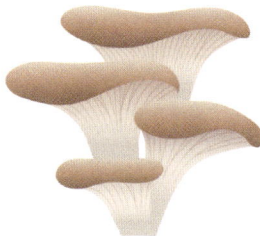

With mushrooms prevention can sometimes be easier than cure: improving your lawn's drainage is a key step in preventing mushrooms from popping up. Read more about this on pages 23–4.

Keeping your lawn clean is another crucial part of preventing mushrooms from popping up. Organic matter like grass clippings, fallen leaves, and animal waste can create a perfect environment for mushrooms to thrive. So, it is important to box clippings and use a rotary mower to pick up all the debris if you want to avoid mushrooms.

Regular feeding is another key strategy in preventing mushrooms from appearing. Mushrooms can be a sign that your lawn needs a nitrogen boost to stay healthy and dense, and a good cure is to increase the nitrogen content with proper fertilizer. Mushrooms often pop up in lawns that are low in nitrogen because they feed on decaying organic matter in the soil - like old roots, leaves, or thatch. When nitrogen is lacking, grass grows more slowly, leaving more organic debris for fungi to break down. Adding nitrogen boosts grass growth, which helps the lawn outcompete mushrooms and speeds up the decomposition of organic material, leaving less fuel for fungi to feed on.

There is one particularly sore subject when it comes to lawn care - weeds. It is a dirty word we all try to avoid. This can sometimes feel like fighting a losing battle and a huge disappointment when you step out to find a couple more weeds have appeared overnight. Fortunately, there are lots of ways to fight back.

Weeds

What are Weeds?

Weeds are not just unsightly intruders in your lawn; they're plants that thrive under the same conditions as your grass. When your lawn is cut too low or the soil is compacted, weeds seize the opportunity to grow. They're opportunistic, taking advantage of any weakness in your lawn's health to establish themselves. This is why a well-maintained, healthy lawn is your best defence against these pesky invaders.

Understanding how weeds work is the first step in effective weed control. Weeds are more than just an eyesore; they're a real nuisance with far-reaching impacts. These unwanted plants compete fiercely with your grass for essential resources like nutrients, sunlight, and water. This competition can significantly diminish your lawn's health and vibrancy.

Some weeds go a step further by releasing chemicals that stunt the growth of surrounding plants, dealing an additional blow to your lawn's well-being.

A weed-infested lawn often signals deeper problems. Poor soil conditions – such as compaction – or improper mowing practices can create an environment where weeds flourish while grass struggles. Understanding these underlying issues is key to maintaining a healthy, weed-resistant lawn.

Before we dive into the common weeds you're likely to find in your lawn, there are a few things to cover as general practice to protect against all unwanted weeds.

The first is density. If your lawn is a lush, dense carpet of grass and you can't see any soil then it's likely weeds are not going to be able to find a place to call home and establish themselves in your lawn, so good overseeding can go a long way towards weed prevention (see pages 76–80).

The second thing is to get the right mowing height for your lawn. As we've previously discussed (see pages 46–47), leaving the lawn to get too long or maintaining it too high actually stops the plant from trying to grow laterally, and therefore makes the base very weak and sparse. On the other hand, having the lawn too short can make weeds incredibly obvious as most weeds are quite low growing.

Finally, you should follow a regular feeding plan to keep the grass plants strong, able to compete with and push out weeds with constant and consistent growth and repair.

Dandelions

This weed is a staple pain in the UK, and one many of you will be familiar with. Dandelions are a particular eyesore in the lawn, and a very obvious uninvited visitor.

Their secret weapon is a deep taproot that digs in and holds on tight, making them tricky to remove completely. Even a tiny piece of root left behind can enable a new plant to sprout, meaning these tenacious intruders often bounce back stronger than ever!

And let's not forget those puffball seeds – one gust of wind and they're off, ready to take over every corner of your lawn!

While they're undeniably resilient and even offer some benefits (like feeding pollinators or aerating soil), dandelions are rarely welcome.

They are particularly hard to prepare for and prevent due to the airborne nature of their seeds, so it all goes back to the principles of a dense, well-fed lawn to shut the door and stop the seeds from taking hold.

If you do find yourself with a dandelion problem, they are quite a solid weed but it is possible to remove by hand with a hand trowel; just make sure you get deep enough to remove all of the taproot.

Clover

Clover in lawns can be a contentious issue. For some, it's a welcome addition, offering a splash of colour and a source of nectar for bees. For others, it's an unwelcome intruder, disrupting the uniformity of a well-kept lawn due to its aggressive growth habit.

Clover spreads rapidly, often outcompeting grass for resources and space. Moreover, its ability to fix nitrogen from the air into the soil can create an imbalance in soil nutrients, favouring itself over other plants. This can lead to a lawn dominated by clover.

Clover can be a persistent issue in lawns, but it's not invincible. The first step in removing clover from your lawn is to understand its growth pattern. Clover spreads quickly, growing laterally, and can easily take over a lawn if left unchecked. It thrives in conditions where grass struggles, such as in poor soil or areas of low nitrogen.

To remove clover, you can start by hand weeding. This method is effective, but can be time-consuming, especially for larger lawns. Use a hand fork or weeding tool to dig out the clover, ensuring you remove the root to prevent regrowth.

Mare's Tail

Mare's tail, also known as horsetail, is a fast-spreading perennial weed that can be an absolute nightmare to control and remove. Recognizable by its tall, feathery, segmented stems, it thrives in a variety of conditions, particularly in damp or poorly drained soils. This ancient plant, dating back to the time of the dinosaurs, has an extensive root system that can reach several metres deep, making it highly resistant to pulling and traditional weed-control methods.

Mare's tail's tough, waxy coating also makes it difficult for many herbicides to penetrate. It also has another secret weapon: if you look to remove it by hand and just snap the stem rather than removing the root, this actually encourages more growth and duplication – no wonder it survived the dinosaurs! As ever prevention through a healthy lawn is the key to avoiding this weed taking root.

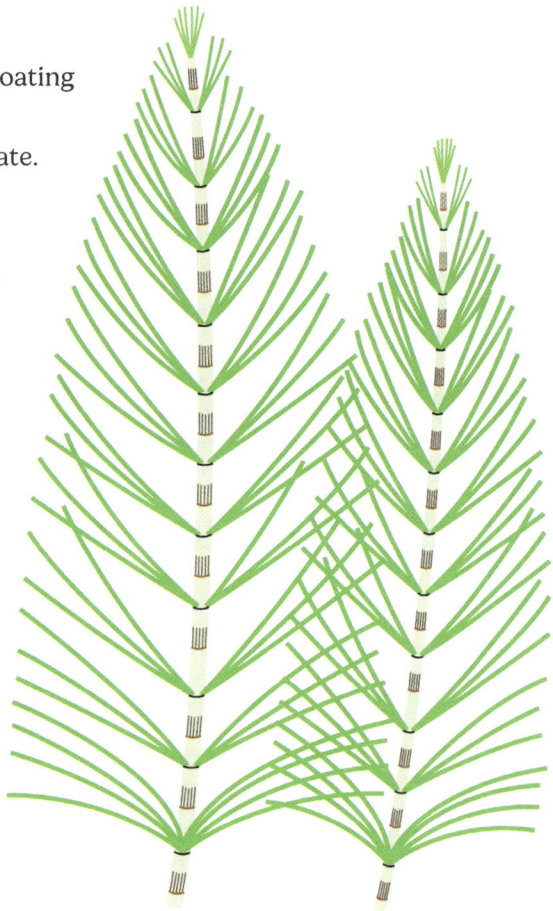

Daisies

This is one of the nicer weeds (if we're allowed to have such a category!) and one many people are quite happy to live with in their lawn. Daisies are fun for children to pick, they make cute daisy chains, and they're not too dense or overpowering. However, daisies are still a weed and if you want your lawn to be grass only, then it's one that needs to leave.

These low-growing plants are tough and adaptable, thriving in compacted soil where grass may struggle. They have a rosette of leaves that hugs the ground, making them resistant to mowing, and difficult to eradicate fully. Once established, daisies can quickly spread, creating clusters that compete with grass for space and nutrients.

On the brighter side, daisies are loved by pollinators like bees and butterflies, and their presence can add a whimsical, natural look to a lawn.

The best way to remove daisies is through the application of herbicide (as a single or double use).

Thistles

Thistles are a very common perennial weed known for their spiky leaves and tall, flowering stems topped with purple blooms. While they may look striking, they're unwelcome guests in most lawns and gardens, due to their invasive nature and ability to spread quickly. Thistles reproduce both through wind-dispersed seeds and creeping roots, making them particularly challenging to control. Their deep taproots allow them to survive drought and resist simple pulling, often regrowing if even a small piece of the root is left behind, just like dandelions.

Regular mowing can help to weaken young thistles in lawns, while targeted herbicidal treatments are often necessary to eliminate established plants. Addressing thistles promptly helps prevent them from taking over and ensures your lawn stays healthy and weed-free.

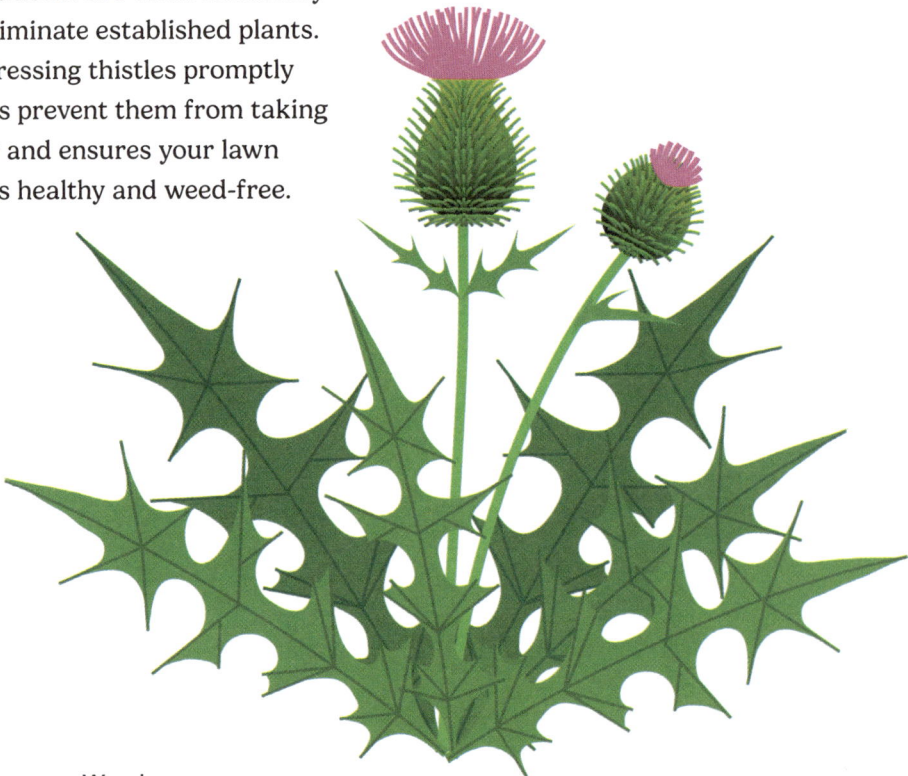

Plantains

The plantain is a solid, hardy perennial weed. There are two main types: broadleaf plantain with wide, rounded leaves and ribwort plantain, which has narrow, lance-shaped leaves. Both types form low-growing rosettes that can withstand mowing and foot traffic, making them difficult to get rid of, and they are very obvious after cutting. Plantain spreads by producing a large number of seeds and thrives in poorly drained or compacted soil. The best way to control them is to improve soil health through aeration, applying selective herbicides to target the weed without damaging the grass or, if you're able to, this is a weed that can be easily removed manually using a hand fork.

Crabgrass

This invasive weed, with its distinct characteristics and survival tactics, can quickly overrun your lawn if not properly managed. It's a type of broadleaved weed that has a distinct appearance, making it relatively easy to identify. The most noticeable characteristic of crabgrass is its long, spindly stems that seem to crawl out of the ground, much like a crab walking across the sand – hence its name.

The weed grows from a single root and is dark green in colour. It grows outwards, creating a clumpy appearance, unlike healthy grass blades that grow upright. Another unique feature of crabgrass is its love for hot, dry conditions. If your lawn has been neglected and the soil is poor, you are likely to see an invasion of this annoying weed. It is aggressive and invasive and, if left unchecked, it can quickly choke out your grass and other native plants.

Crabgrass also has a knack for survival. Each plant produces thousands of seeds that can remain dormant in the soil for years. This means that even if you manage to get rid of the visible crabgrass, you're still at risk of a resurgence from the seeds left behind.

Chickweed

Chickweed is a fast-growing annual weed that thrives in cool, damp conditions, often appearing in lawns, borders, and bare patches of soil. Recognizable by its small, oval leaves and delicate, star-shaped white flowers, chickweed can spread rapidly by producing a large number of seeds that remain viable in the soil for years. It also has creeping stems that root as they touch the ground, allowing it to form dense mats that compete with surrounding plants for nutrients and moisture. While shallow-rooted and relatively easy to pull out, chickweed's ability to regrow quickly means it is important to remove it before it seeds. Regular weeding and improving soil drainage can help to keep this common weed under control.

Solutions

Herbicides

A herbicide is a man-made chemical product used to control or eliminate unwanted weeds. Herbicides are typically classified as either selective or non-selective.

- **Selective herbicides** are formulated to target specific weeds without harming your grass, making them ideal for lawn care. They work by exploiting differences in the biology of weeds and grass. For example, some selective herbicides disrupt processes unique to broadleaved plants, such as their ability to produce certain proteins or enzymes essential for growth. Others may interfere with photosynthesis or hormone regulation in the target weed. It's quite impressive science!

- **Non-selective herbicides** will kill any vegetation they come into contact with, and are best suited for clearing unwanted growth in areas where no plants are desired. The most common non-selective is glyphosate (see page opposite).

Effective use of herbicides requires careful application at the right time. Generally, using herbicides in months when weeds are actively growing will give a much better success rate.

Glyphosate

Glyphosate – a word that strikes fear within the gardening world – is a broad-spectrum herbicide and its primary role is to control a wide variety of weeds.

It is a chemical compound that has been created and tweaked over time to control persistent and invasive weeds, such as the ones mentioned in this chapter. Glyphosate works by targeting enzymes essential for plant growth, effectively destroying the entire plant, including the roots, which means it must be licensed and companies need to be registered to produce it, as its use involves killing a living organism.

While glyphosate is powerful, it's also non-selective, meaning it can harm any plant it touches – which also means your lawn! If you were to spray glyphosate over your lawn, you'd find that in a matter of days you will no longer have one.

! **While glyphosate might be much too harmful and risky to use as part of your general lawn-care practice, it can have a role within the garden, such as in those areas in which you are looking for no plant growth, such as barked paths.**

Alternatively, if you're looking to start a lawn from scratch an application of glyphosate before starting the project means everything can be killed off and no old or foreign grasses or weeds will be breaking out in your new lawn. It is best to apply this roughly 7-10 days before beginning new projects, but always refer to the manufacturer's instructions for full guidance.

This is not exactly the subject that comes to mind when thinking about sunny days spent in the garden, but unfortunately it is a necessary one. With all the different variables a lawn has to deal with, it's likely that at some point diseases are going to creep in and take hold. Disease can come in a variety of forms, and range from unsightly to quite disastrous but, fear not, not there is often a solution.

Diseases

Red Thread

Red thread is a fungal disease that can damage the appearance of your lawn. It is a common problem for homeowners, especially during humid times of the year. This disease gets its name from the red or pink threads that grow on infected grass blades.

Red thread is a lawn disease that is caused by a fungal pathogen called *Laetisaria fuciformis*. The fungus thrives in cool, moist environments, and can survive in the soil for long periods. The disease often appears in patches and initially presents as small, circular, pink-coloured patches in the lawn. As the disease progresses, the patches can grow and merge together, forming larger areas of discoloured grass.

The good news is that red thread is not a deadly disease and can be treated with proper lawn care practices. The first step in removing red thread is to fertilize your lawn with nitrogen-rich fertilizer. This will help to promote healthy growth and the recovery of the infected grass. You should also make sure you water your lawn thoroughly but infrequently to prevent the disease from spreading. Avoid watering your lawn in the evening as this can create a moist environment that creates ideal conditions for the fungus to grow.

Another effective way of removing red thread is by physically removing the infected grass. This is especially necessary for severely infected areas. You can do this by mowing your lawn and collecting the clippings. This will help to remove the fungus spores and prevent them from spreading.

Fusarium Patch

Fusarium patch is a disease caused by the fungus *Microdochium nivale*, which is naturally present in most lawns. In the right weather conditions, the spores become active and create patches of yellow-brown grass, which will stay dry even when dew is present in the mornings.

On close inspection, you may notice small white fibres of white or pink mould, resembling cotton wool on top of the patch. These signs of mould are the key indicator that the damage is indeed a result of fusarium patch. If you don't see any signs of mould, try covering a patch overnight: if mould does not appear by the morning, the discoloration is likely not a result of fusarium.

Fusarium patch spores are present in most lawns all year round, as they are easily carried by the wind, and are often present in the soil, where they help decompose dead matter and maintain a healthy balance. However, they are only identifiable when they become active and cause damage to your lawn.

This disease develops during autumn and winter when conditions are mild and wet, daylight hours are limited, and there is less air movement. Fusarium patch is also known as 'snow mould', as it often occurs while the lawn is covered in snow, which creates a layer of insulation for the grass. Fusarium is mostly seen in lawns that are weak and stressed, mown very short, or newly laid. Healthy, established lawns are less likely to suffer from the disease.

Because the spores of fusarium patch have a very short incubation period, a lawn that shows no apparent sign of disease one minute can exhibit extensive fusarium issues the next. Dry, brown spots can appear and grow rapidly, often overnight.

Fusarium patch may well go away on its own, when the weather conditions change, and the temperatures drop. Winter frost is an effective remedy against fusarium patch. The brown patches left behind will naturally right themselves through the next growing season, although re-seeding may be necessary if the damage has been extensive.

Fungicide can be used to treat fusarium patch, but it will need to be applied by a professional and often one application is not enough.

The best way to keep fusarium patch and other diseases at bay is to keep your lawn healthy, which will help it overcome and outgrow diseases. Mow your lawn regularly, and use aeration and scarification to maintain your soil in the best shape. In addition, make sure you use the right feed for your lawn through the year. In the autumn, you'll need a low-nitrogen and high-potassium feed to promote growth and strengthen the plant.

If you have noticed the disease appearing on your lawn, try to avoid walking on the grass, to avoid spreading the spores to other areas. Similarly, avoid mowing your lawn or creating any further stress that might weaken the plant. But if you do need to mow your lawn, make sure you clean your lawn mower and the blades thoroughly once you are finished, to avoid re-contaminating the lawn later on.

Fairy Rings

These sound a lot friendlier than they are. Fairy rings are a common lawn issue caused by soil-dwelling fungi that form circular patterns of discoloured grass or mushrooms.

These rings can appear as fairly dark green patches, areas of dead or thinning grass, or circles of mushrooms, depending on the species and soil conditions. The fungi decompose organic matter in the soil, releasing nitrogen, which can cause the grass within the ring to grow more vigorously or, conversely, die off due to the build-up of hydrophobic (or water-repellant) substances.

Fairy rings are most noticeable in well-established lawns and can vary greatly in size, from small rings that are a few centimetres wide to large ones spanning several metres. The rings often expand outwards over time, as the fungus spreads through the soil.

Key signs to look out for include unusually lush grass growth or dry, dead patches that seem resistant to watering, with mushrooms sometimes forming at the edges.

There is no simple cure for fairy rings because the fungi live deep in the soil and can persist for years. Fungicides are generally ineffective against them. However, you can manage fairy rings by improving soil aeration and drainage, removing thatch, and using wetting agents to help water penetrate the soil. Maintaining healthy lawn care practices, regular watering, feeding, and mowing, also supports grass recovery and helps minimize the visible effects.

Dollar Spot

Dollar spot is a common fungal disease that can affect lawns, particularly during warm, humid conditions or when the grass is under stress. Its name comes from the small, circular patches of straw-coloured grass it creates, roughly the size of a silver coin. These patches often appear scattered across the lawn and, if left untreated, can merge into larger areas of discoloured and weakened turf.

The disease is caused by the fungus *Clarireedia*, which thrives in mild temperatures of around 12–30°C (54–86°F), high humidity, and prolonged periods of leaf wetness.

Lawns that are undernourished, especially those lacking in nitrogen, are particularly susceptible to dollar spot. This disease is also more likely to appear if the grass is mowed too short or if watering practices leave the lawn damp for extended periods. The fungus spreads easily through spores carried by wind, water, or foot traffic, making prevention an important part of lawn care.

To manage dollar spot, start by focusing on lawn health. Ensuring your grass receives adequate nutrients, particularly nitrogen, will help it stay strong and resilient. Watering thoroughly but less frequently, preferably in the early morning, can also reduce the moisture conditions that the fungus needs to thrive. Avoid watering in the evening, as this can leave the grass damp overnight, and encourage fungal growth.

Take-all Patch

Take-all patch is a fungal disease that primarily affects turf grass, particularly bentgrass, making it a common concern for lawns, golf courses, and other areas with fine turf. The disease is caused by the fungus *Gaeumannomyces graminis* var. *avenae*, which attacks the roots and lower stems of grass plants. It typically appears as circular patches of brown or straw-coloured grass that gradually expand over time, leaving behind thin, weakened turf. The affected patches often have a reddish or bronze tinge at the edges, particularly in their early stages, and can merge to form larger, irregular areas of damaged grass.

This disease thrives in cool, wet conditions and is most active during the spring and autumn when soil moisture is high. Take-all patch is often associated with alkaline soils, poor drainage, and lawns under stress from improper maintenance. Grass that has been recently established or overseeded is especially vulnerable, as the fungus can exploit the weakened root systems.

Managing take-all patch requires a combination of practices to improve soil health and reduce the conditions that favour the fungus. Start by addressing the soil's pH level, as the disease thrives in alkaline soils (any PH level over 7). Applying acidifying agents, such as sulphur-based products, can help lower the pH and create an environment less hospitable to the fungus. Improving drainage through aeration or adding organic matter to the soil will also reduce waterlogging and promote stronger root systems.

Proper fertilization is key to preventing and managing take-all patch. Applying a balanced fertilizer with adequate levels of nitrogen, phosphorus, and potassium will support healthy grass growth and improve its resistance to disease. Avoid over-fertilizing, as this can stress the grass and worsen the problem. Watering thoroughly but infrequently, and only in the early morning, will help to maintain soil moisture without creating overly wet conditions that encourage fungal activity.

Anthracnose

Anthracnose is a fungal disease caused by *Colletotrichum cereale*, affecting turf grass such as *Poa annua* (annual meadow grass, see page 14) and bentgrass. Anthracnose can appear as a foliar blight, which is yellowing and browning of leaves, or as a basal rot, which is where the crown and roots of the plant become dark and brittle.

This disease thrives in stressed lawns. In particular this happens during warm, humid weather or when grass is undernourished or cut too short.

To manage anthracnose, start by reducing the stress on your lawn. Avoid mowing too low, ensure your grass receives adequate nutrients, particularly nitrogen, and water thoroughly but less frequently. Improving drainage and aerating the soil can also help prevent fungal development.

For severe cases, fungicides labelled for anthracnose can be used, but maintaining a healthy, well-fed lawn is the best long-term defence against this disease.

Solutions

Fungicides

Fungicides are treatments designed to prevent or manage fungal diseases in your lawn, helping to protect grass from damage caused by harmful fungi. They work by either killing the fungus or stopping its growth, depending on the type of product used. While fungicides can be effective, they are most successful when combined with good lawn-care practices, as healthy grass is naturally more resistant to disease.

There are two main types of fungicides: preventative and curative.

- **Preventative fungicides** are applied before signs of disease appear, creating a barrier that stops fungi from infecting the grass.

- **Curative fungicides**, on the other hand, are used after a disease has taken hold, helping to slow or stop its spread.

Most fungicides come in liquid or granular form and need to be applied evenly across the lawn, often requiring multiple treatments for lasting results.

When using fungicides, timing is critical. Many fungal diseases thrive in specific weather conditions, such as warm, humid periods, so applying fungicides early – before conditions become ideal for fungi – can make a big difference.

! **Always follow the product's instructions carefully, including recommended application rates and safety precautions.**

Overusing fungicides can lead to resistance in fungi and harm beneficial organisms in your lawn's ecosystem.

It is also important to remember that fungicides are not a cure-all. They work best as part of an integrated approach that includes proper mowing, watering, aeration, and fertilization. By focusing on the overall health of your lawn, you'll reduce the likelihood of fungal problems and the need for fungicides in the first place.

While we're dealing with the uninspiring, difficult topics of lawn care, it's time to look at the unwanted creatures that can make gardens such hard work. Now, most of us can cope with a few worm casts or the occasional bird pecking but pests, on the other hand, can wreak havoc and kill off a good lawn in no time at all. Spotting problems early is crucial, but unfortunately controlling pests in the current climate is quite tricky.

Garden
Pests

Chafer Grubs

Although it is not always easy to tell, your garden provides a home to many forms of life, including fungi, insects, and small animals. The soil provides the perfect environment for chafer beetles to lay their eggs, which eventually develop into chafer grubs.

Chafer grubs are the immature larvae of chafer beetles. The adults emerge in early summer and survive for about two to three weeks. During this time, they are harmless to your lawn, but they may lay eggs in the soil, which hatch into tiny larvae during the summer. The grubs are soil-dwelling creatures that feed on plant roots and other forms of organic matter in your soil. In the winter months they lay dormant and burrowed deep in the soil, re-emerging in the spring, when they live and feed in the more superficial layers of soil. Chafer beetles have a life cycle lasting between one to three years, depending on the species. During this time, the larvae (chafer grubs) live in the soil feeding on roots.

Chafers are long, stout, creamy coloured creatures with a light brown head and three pairs of distinctive legs attached close to the head. Their bodies are curved in a C-shape, and they are bigger than adult beetles, measuring anywhere between 10 mm (⅜ in) and 15 mm (⅔ in) when grown. They cause similar damage to leatherjackets (see pages 154–157) and other root-eating grubs. A lawn in good health, with a strong root system, can survive minor infestations of chafer grubs with minor consequences to its overall well-being. However, in the case of more serious infestations, chafer grubs can cause serious damage. As the roots of your lawn are weakened by the grubs, you may notice yellowish or bald patches appearing, and if you lift the grass your turf may simply peel away due to the damaged roots.

Your lawn may also be seriously damaged as birds, foxes, badgers, and other animals dig into the soil to feed on the protein-rich larvae. If you are seeing a lot of bird activity this might be a sign that your lawn is currently affected with a chafer problem.

Chafer infestations don't follow any particular pattern; they may appear in your garden but not in a neighbouring garden, or they can be a problem one year and not the next. Generally, newly cultivated ground or neglected weedy gardens are more prone to chafer grubs.

Solutions

How to Treat Chafer Grubs

There are no legal chemicals available on the UK market or in most of Europe to treat chafer infestations. In the USA, products containing imidacloprid or chlorantraniliprole are available for home use in some states; however there is a general preference for no-pesticide solutions.

One treatment option that is readily available is nematodes. You can buy nematodes, which are natural parasites that latch on to the grubs and kill them. This method is fairly expensive and, as nematodes are living organisms, they need to be used within a few weeks of purchase or they will die. Moreover, due to all the factors that need to be perfect, the success rate is unsurprisingly low.

An alternative method:

Night removal of chafer grubs

You can remove chafer grubs in a rather grim process that brings them to the surface overnight. This technique is particularly popular on golf greens and sports surfaces where performance is paramount.

Water your lawn well in the evening and cover the surface with a plastic sheet, blankets, rugs, or any other available covering. This will encourage the grubs to move to the surface of the lawn during the night.

Remove the covers at dawn the next morning and let the birds and mammals that visit your garden take care of the problem for you by feasting on the grubs, or use a brush and remove them all yourself.

This is an unpleasant sight to wake up to, but it is certainly an effective method of removal.

Leatherjackets

Leatherjackets is the common name for the larvae of crane flies. These creatures are often mistaken for chafer grubs. They are typically greyish brown in colour, with a cylindrical body shape.

Their size can vary, but they usually measure about 2.5 cm (1 in) in length. Unlike many other insects, leatherjackets do not have legs or a distinct head. This feature often confuses people, leading to misidentification. The skin of these pests is tough and leathery, hence the name 'leatherjacket'. This tough exterior helps them survive in various conditions, making them quite a resilient pest.

The life cycle of leatherjackets begins with the laying of eggs in late summer or early autumn. The eggs hatch into larvae after two to three weeks and, after feeding on grass roots and growing during the winter and spring, they pupate within the soil. Then, in late summer, the adults crane flies emerge and are ready to start the cycle all over again. Understanding this cycle is not just a matter of curiosity, but a crucial step in minimizing the damage they can do by tackling them at the right time.

Spotting a leatherjacket problem is much the same as for chafer grubs, as they are similar in a number of ways. A yellowing lawn, animal activity, or weak roots are the signs you want to be on the alert for. You may also notice that the surface of your lawn feels spongy underfoot. This is due to the tunnels created by the leatherjackets as they move around beneath the surface of the lawn.

Solutions

There are two main strategies to control leatherjackets: biological control (using nematodes) and chemical control.

Biological Controls – Nematodes

Nematodes are microscopic, soil-dwelling worms that naturally target and kill leatherjacket larvae. Once applied to moist soil, they actively seek out the larvae, enter their bodies, and release bacteria that kill the host within a few days. Nematodes are safe for humans, pets, and wildlife, and can be a highly effective and environmentally friendly solution when applied correctly – typically in late summer or early autumn, when leatherjacket larvae are most vulnerable. For best results, keep the lawn well-watered after application to maintain soil moisture.

Chemical Control

If nematodes are not practical or effective in your situation, chemical controls are available. These should be used with care to avoid harming beneficial organisms and the broader environment.

Pesticides

Chemical pesticides may be used to manage leatherjackets, with insecticides offering the most targeted solution. These products are formulated specifically to kill insect larvae like leatherjackets. Broader-spectrum pesticides may also be effective, particularly if you're dealing with multiple pest issues.

! Chemical control methods should be used responsibly. Always follow the manufacturer's instructions and consider the potential impact on non-target species and the wider environment. Implementing effective control measures is key, but it's equally important to do so in a way that minimizes harm to the planet.

PREVENTION IS KEY

When it comes to your lawn, prevention is always cheaper and more effective than cure. As with many other problems, maintaining a healthy lawn that can recuperate quickly is the most effective way of reducing damage. A heavily managed lawn is less likely to develop grub infestations, so regular lawn-care practices and treatment with an iron sulphate-rich feed is a cost-effective way of strengthening your lawn, and will help prevent infestations.

Ants

Ants are a common sight in many gardens and, while they can be beneficial, an overpopulation can lead to several issues. These tiny creatures can disrupt the beauty of your lawn with their ant hills and potentially cause damage to your grass. However, they can be beneficial in helping to break down organic material, improving soil fertility and structure. Their tunnels can also aid in aerating the soil, which as we know can be hugely beneficial to lawn health.

Ants become a problem when their activities start to interfere with the look and feel of your lawn, mainly when ants build their nests, resulting in ant hills or mounds. Furthermore, a large ant population can cause significant root damage as they nest underground, constructing intricate labyrinths in the root systems. This can lead to weakened grass, making it more susceptible to diseases and other pests.

To start the process of ant control, you'll first need to locate the ant nest in your lawn. This might seem like a daunting task, but it's actually quite straightforward. Ants are social insects, and they usually leave trails leading back to their nest.

There are a few natural solutions we'd recommend trying first.

Raking ant hills is a simple yet effective method to control ants in your lawn. This technique disrupts the ants' habitat, forcing them to relocate and reducing their population in your garden. However, it's essential to rake regularly as ants can rebuild their colonies quickly.

Dish soap can be an effective, natural method to control ants in your lawn. A solution of three per cent dish soap mixed with water can be sprayed over the infested area. To enhance the effectiveness of this solution, you can add a spoonful of vegetable oil, but don't do this when the sun is at its highest or you'll cook the lawn, literally.

Nematodes are microscopic creatures that act as parasites on other insects, including ants. They are an effective way to control pests in your lawn without causing damage to your grass.

Chilli pepper is regarded by some gardeners as an effective method of ant control, but this is still up for debate.

If you're dealing with a severe ant infestation in your lawn, strong chemical ant killers can be effective. These come in various forms, including powders, liquids, sprays, and gels or baits designed to eliminate ants quickly and help you regain control of your lawn.

While chemical treatments can provide a fast solution, they should be used as a last resort. It's always best to try natural methods first and only turn to chemical alternatives when necessary.

Earthworms

When earthworms are active in the superficial layer of the soil, especially in the wetter seasons, you may notice small piles of soil, also known as worm casts, appearing on your lawn. Worm casts are tiny heaps of soil that appear as a result of earthworm activity; they are the nutrient-rich remains of the worm's digestive process, as it feeds on organic matter within the soil. There are a myriad of species of earthworm in the world but of the thirty-one found in the UK, only three create worm casts.

Although worm casts can be a nuisance, as they affect the aesthetic appearance of your lawn, they are actually extremely beneficial. Not only do they comprise nutrient-rich matter, but the worm activity that creates them improves soil structure, encourages microbial activity and decomposition, breaks down thatch, and provides natural aeration to your lawn.

In lawns that are kept long, it is fairly easy to brush off dry worm casts, and incorporate them back into the grass. Let the casts dry before breaking them up by using a wire rake or stiff brush and dispersing them across the lawn. This will get rid of the casts and allow the nutrient-rich matter back into your soil.

Dealing with worm casts is harder on fine, short, mown lawns. This process can also be tricky when the weather is damp or wet, as the casts do not have a chance to dry. When the casts are squashed, the muddy smear they leave behind can be quite visible on short lawns, and it creates an ideal bed for weed seeds and mosses to become established.

During autumn and spring, when there is a lot of worm activity, try to keep off the lawn to avoid additional smearing and spreading of the casts. You can also try keeping your lawn longer during these periods of the year to avoid the aesthetic problem of worm casts. As earthworm activity is so beneficial, if it is possible to tolerate earthworm casts, it is a good idea to do so.

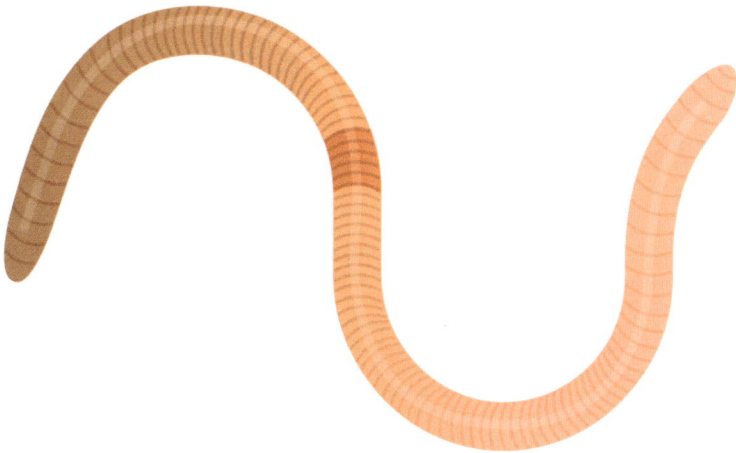

Lawns have a huge effect on our planet, and the environment also has a huge effect on the way our lawns perform. With the climate change our world is facing, lawns can absolutely benefit the environment by helping to provide oxygen and natural drainage. We must also recognize that the seasons we are used to are starting to blend together, and lawn care needs to take a more reactive approach.

Environmental Impact

Impacting the Air

We hope you will be interested to hear that our lawns help to produce the oxygen we need to live and breathe – and it's harder to get more important than that. A key process that occurs during photosynthesis, as grass absorbs sunlight, is that it uses carbon dioxide (CO_2) from the air and water from the soil to create energy, releasing oxygen as a by-product.

Grass is the third-biggest source of oxygen on Earth after trees and algae, and an average lawn produces enough oxygen for a family of four every day.

Conversely, lawns also absorb CO_2, which means the greater the area of lawn we have, the more we are doing to help slow the impact of climate change.

Seasons are Changing

The traditional four seasons of spring, summer, autumn, and winter are starting to merge together and overlap. Not only is the changing of each season becoming harder to spot, but the peaks and troughs are becoming more extreme. For example, the weather in the UK is unpredictable at the best of times, but without the structure and reliability of the four seasons, it is now affecting the way we plan and approach lawn care.

Changes to our seasons mean we have to be much more flexible, utilize expertise, and use common sense to guide us through the year with regards to feeding, formulations, and undertaking lawn-care practices.

Heatwaves

Lawns play a significant role in mitigating the effects of heatwaves by staying much cooler than hardstanding surfaces like concrete, tarmac, or stone. Grass has a natural cooling effect due to a process called evapotranspiration, which is where water evaporates back into the atmosphere from the grass blades and soil, lowering the surrounding air temperature. This cooling effect can reduce the urban heat island (UHI) effect, where cities experience significantly higher temperatures than rural areas, due to the abundance of heat-absorbing surfaces. In fact, studies show that grass-covered areas can be up to 15°C (59°F) cooler than paved surfaces on a hot day. By absorbing less heat and radiating less warmth back into the atmosphere, lawns not only provide cooling systems but also contribute to reducing our energy consumption, such as air-conditioning use, thereby indirectly helping to counter climate change.

Maintaining green spaces in urban environments is a crucial strategy for adapting to rising global temperatures while offering a natural and sustainable way to cool our surroundings.

Flooding

Unfortunately, with climate change and as we continue to develop our cities, flooding is becoming more common. Climate change brings heavier and more unpredictable rainfall, overwhelming our drainage systems and natural waterways. At the same time, cities are expanding, with more hardstanding surfaces like roads, pavements, and buildings replacing permeable ground. These surfaces prevent rainwater from soaking into the ground, causing it to run off quickly and increasing the risk of surface-water flooding.

This is where your lawn comes in to combat flooding, and stay strong against the risk of it. Grass has a fantastic way of absorbing water and with good, aerated soil, water can permeate through your lawn extremely quickly. The more grass we have, the better chance there is of reducing the impact of flooding.

Artificial Lawns

The age-old debate between natural and artificial lawns is still ongoing. While artificial lawns have gained a lot of popularity in recent years, we are not sure they are the future.

Artificial lawns are made from synthetic plastics woven into a plastic backing and laid in a garden on a base of compacted grit sand. The materials used are not biodegradable and can take hundreds of years to decompose at the end of their life. Additionally, the production and transportation of artificial lawns contribute to the carbon footprint. They also give nothing back to our environment, in terms of either oxygen production or carbon absorption, like a real, living lawn will do.

We accept that artifical lawns can have their uses, such as for pitches where people can now enjoy a sport all year round, and they can be a nice source of green in the garden, especially in areas where it is a struggle to get grass to grow or for people for whom the physical work of maintaining a lawn is not possible.

If there is ever a choice, however, we definitely know which side we're on.

Pollinators

You may think that grasses in your lawn, especially those prevented from flowering due to regular mowing, are not as important to wildlife and pollinators as garden flowering plants, but this isn't the case. Grass provides cover and shelter for insects like beetles, ants, and grasshoppers, which are important parts of the food chain. These insects, in turn, attract birds, hedgehogs, and other small mammals that forage for food in lawns. The soil underneath a lawn also supports a rich ecosystem of small creatures, hosting earthworms and microorganisms that improve soil health and provide sustenance for larger creatures.

Now, if you wanted to go further and do more for bees, butterflies, and other small creatures, then we would definitely recommend looking for less used sections of lawn to transform into wildflower areas. This way you'll be able to provide the flowering plants that pollinators need, without increasing the maintenance of your lawn or garden too much, while also creating a beautiful backdrop.

Trends in Lawn Styles

In recent years, there has been growing interest in alternatives to the traditional grass lawn. Options like clover, chamomile, wildflower mixes, and even a blend of grass and common weeds are becoming more visible in gardens across the world. These approaches tend to focus on lower maintenance and boosting biodiversity and, for some gardeners, they offer an appealing change of pace.

Clover lawns, for example, stay green in dry weather and require less mowing, while chamomile lawns offer a fragrant and softer ground cover suited to lighter foot traffic. Wildflower lawns aim to replicate natural meadows, encouraging pollinators and adding visual variety. Some people even opt to let grass mix freely with low-growing weeds such as daisies or dandelions, embracing a wilder and relaxed aesthetic.

That said, these options do come with trade-offs, whether these are durability, year-round appearance, or how well your lawn stands up to children, pets, and everyday use. Traditional grass lawns remain the go-to choice for those wanting a classic, versatile, and reliable surface that looks smart and feels great underfoot.

We believe in the value of a well-kept grass lawn, but it's good to understand the full landscape of what is out there. After all, the more you know, the better choices you can make for your garden.

Every great lawn starts with the right tools and knowing how to use them. While you don't need to go and buy everything on offer from the local DIY shop, having a few well-chosen essentials can make lawn care quicker, easier, and far more effective. We'll walk you through the must-haves for any lawn enthusiast, from the basics like spades and rakes, to the more specialist kit like scarifiers and edging tools. Whether you're starting from scratch or upgrading what you've already got, we'll help you build a reliable, no-fuss tool shed that gets the job done. After all, a good lawn is only as good as the tools behind it.

Tool
Shed

BLOWER (ABOVE)

A powered tool (electric or petrol) that produces a strong air stream to clear leaves, grass clippings, and debris from paths and lawns.

EDGING IRON/HALF-MOON LAWN EDGER

A flat, semicircular blade with a long handle, used to create clean, precise edges along lawns, paths, and flower beds.

EDGING SHEARS

Long-handled shears with horizontal blades, designed for trimming and shaping lawn edges neatly.

FORK

A garden tool with long, sturdy tines, ideal for loosening compacted soil, aerating lawns, and turning compost.

GERMINATION SHEET

A breathable, moisture-retaining cover placed over newly seeded areas to speed up germination and protect seeds from birds.

HAND FORK

A small, three- or four-pronged tool used for loosening soil, weeding, and aerating around plants.

HAND TROWEL

A small, pointed digging tool perfect for planting, transplanting, and breaking up soil in flower beds and containers.

HAY RAKE (BELOW)

A large, sturdy rake , also called a landscaping rake, with wide-spaced tines, designed for gathering hay or grass into rows for drying.

HOSE/SPRINKLER

A flexible tube that delivers water over a distance; often attached to a sprinkler for even lawn and garden irrigation.

LAWN MOWER

A motorized tool, usually with rotating blades, that cuts grass to a consistent height, keeping lawns tidy and healthy.

LUTE

A flat-bladed tool on a long handle (see pages 74-5), primarily used to level and smooth soil, gravel, or top dressing.

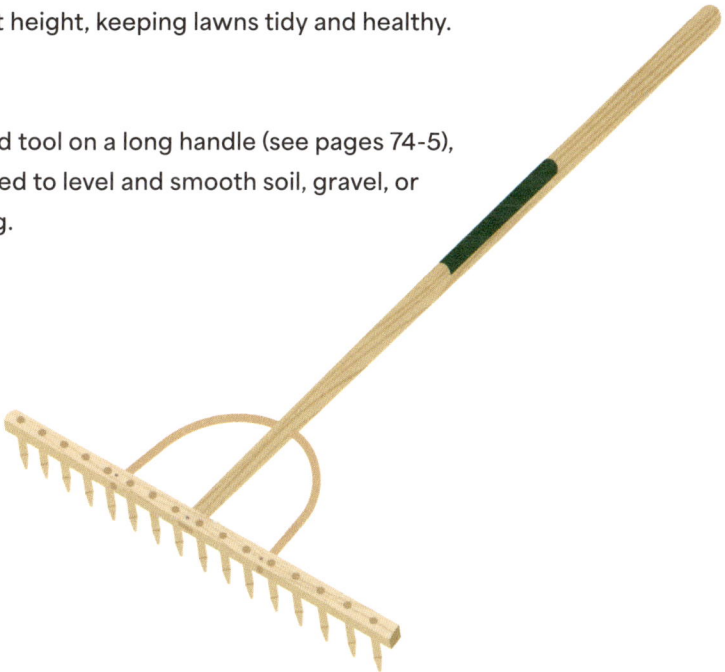

ROLLER

A cylindrical, weighted tool (often filled with water or sand) that compacts soil or smooths out newly laid turf for even growth.

SCARIFIER

A tool (manual or powered) that removes moss, thatch, and dead organic material from the surface of the lawn, helping grass grow more thickly and healthily.

SHOVEL

A broad-bladed tool with a curved edge, used for lifting and moving soil, gravel, mulch, and top dressing.

SPADE

A flat-bladed digging tool with a long handle, used for cutting into soil and turf, edging, and transplanting plants.

SPRING RAKE (RIGHT)

A flexible, fan-shaped rake with thin metal or plastic tines, designed for gathering leaves, grass clippings, and other light debris.

SPRAYER

A handheld, backpack, or wheeled device that applies liquid fertilizers, pesticides, or herbicides evenly over plants and lawns.

STRIMMER (ABOVE)

A powered tool with a rotating nylon line or blade, used to trim grass and weeds in areas a lawn mower can't reach.

WATERING CAN

A portable container with a spout, used for manually watering plants, typically with a detachable rose for gentle water flow.

WHEELBARROW

A wheeled cart with handles (see page 20), used for transporting soil, compost, plants, and garden tools with ease.

If you have a clear plan to follow, caring for your lawn throughout the year doesn't have to be overwhelming. Our seasonal calendar is a rough guide for the key jobs to focus on in each season, helping you maintain a healthy, vibrant lawn no matter the time of year. It's important to remember that weather conditions can vary significantly depending on where you live, and no guide can account for every scenario. Use common sense and keep a close eye on your lawn's unique needs — whether there is an unusually wet spring, a drought-prone summer, or an unexpected early frost, adjusting your approach based on the climate is crucial for success.

Calendar

Spring Essentials

The evenings are longer, the daffodils are in bloom, and there are reasons to be cheerful with all that's happening in the garden. Spring is the perfect time to get your garden 'summer ready' – with a few key jobs and some time with the sleeves rolled up, your lawn will emerge from the winter lull and start to thrive.

START TO CUT

The grass is prepped and the blades are sharpened – now you're ready to cut. Mow your grass shorter week by week. If you go for a severe trim, you risk leaving bald patches (called 'scalping'). A great height to aim for at this time of year is 15–25 mm (⅖–1 in).

The more regularly you can cut during the 'growing season', the better. Every three to four days will encourage the grass to grow thicker and healthier. A lovely striped lawn will be the envy of your neighbours, but it will also be healthier as you get a more consistent cut, and you'll stop the grass from 'laying over'.

The grass bent away from the sun looks bright as it reflects. The grass seems darker facing the sun as it casts a shadow. You get an impressive stripe by cutting in two different directions with a lawn mower with a roller (these are usually petrol powered).

Diagonal lines make your garden look bigger. In irregular spaces, use the contours of the garden and create curved lines. The possibilities are endless – play around until you find something that works.

SCARIFY

Now that it's warmer, you'll want to remove the dead leaves sitting on your lawn, soaking up the sunshine and suffocating your grass. Use a rake (or a scarifier) to clear your lawn of the moss and debris that has built up over the winter. (See pages 58–63 for more information on scarifying.)

AERATE

Over the winter, your lawn will become cold, wet, and compacted, so the roots can't access the nutrients. It is time to aerate now that the soil is now warm enough to penetrate but still moist enough to work with. The roots will then fill the air pockets and start to get the nutrients they need for sustainable growth in the warmer months. (See pages 64–71 for more information on aeration.)

OVERSEED

The stressful winter period will no doubt have seen off some of the weaker plants in your lawn, and you'll start to notice when the rest of the lawn starts to grow. Now is a great time to introduce new growth for the season ahead, replace those dead plants, and build out a thick dense lawn while you have the temperatures needed for growth and still some rainfall for watering. (See pages 76–80 for more information on overseeding.)

FEED

You've scarified and aerated, which means now is a great time to add a feed to help the grass plants recover from the stress of winter, then these two processes can kick-start growth as you come into summer.

Summer Essentials

Summer's when your lawn does the hard graft – long days, dry spells, and plenty of trampling: from kids' football to garden parties. Now's the time to keep your maintenance ticking over with regular mowing, feeding, watering when needed, and keeping an eye out for dry patches or weeds. A bit of care now and then keeps your lawn looking tidy and helps it to bounce back come autumn time.

REMOVE WEEDS

Weeds come into your garden because they are able to take over thin or bare patches quickly. To get your garden into shape, start with a clear-out, and for this you have two options: use a trowel or hand pick weeds (wear gloves and remove the roots); or use a herbicidal weed killer. We believe the trick is to remove them by hand, so you know they are gone.

You might have noticed a bright lime-green grass popping up in your garden at this time of year. Annual meadow grass *(Poa annua)* is very common in the UK, but not easy to get rid of. Unfortunately there isn't an easy treatment or cure, but we would recommend keeping your lawn short and well scarified in summer to counteract its growth.

FIX DAMAGE

If the kids' paddling pool has been out for a day or two, use a rake to stand the grass back up. Grass is a hardy plant, and it should return to a natural, healthy green colour quickly.

If the paddling pool has been there for a few weeks, the turf underneath will have died. You can revive the grass by scarifying (working back and forth with a rake to clear dead grass, weeds, and moss) the discoloured patch and doing a light top-dressing and overseeding. The grass will show signs of recovery in a week, and it will grow again in two to three weeks. (See pages 72–3 for more information on top-dressing.)

KEEP FEEDING

We feed our bodies with the right nutrients to stay fit and healthy, and the same applies if you want a healthy and happy lawn. With warmer weather and plenty of sunshine, we want to maximize a healthy topcoat.

You want to make sure the lawn has a high quantity of nitrogen through the summer to keep the colour and take the wear and tear of summer activities. If you can add a wetting agent in as well this will go a long way to protecting the lawn against heat stress.

WATER

Like all the plants in your garden, the grass is susceptible to drought. Over the summer, look for brown patches on your lawn, which is a sign of drought stress. With increased heat and a lack of water, the root system struggles, and the grass loses its healthy green finish.

For a well-established grass, you should be watering it fairly regularly in the summer. If your lawn looks brown and dried out, you can use a garden fork to create pockets of air beneath the soil and, when you get the hosepipe out, the water will fill the space to help the water reach deeper.

We know it's hard to believe right now, but even in the UK you'll need to water your lawn sometimes. As mentioned above, use a lawn feed with a wetting agent; this will help your grass take in nutrients, guards against plant stress, and stops dried-out areas developing. In between feeds keep watering your lawn if it hasn't rained for a week or more.

TOP TIP: In summer many people cut their lawn more frequently. Whether that's three times a week or even every single day: there's no such thing as cutting too much during this season!

ENJOY YOUR LAWN

It's easy to overlook the simple pleasure of feeling healthy, springy grass between your toes. Summer, or 'growing season' as it is often called, is the most enjoyable time of the year. Whether you're enjoying an ice-cold drink, entertaining friends, or playing football in your garden, we can now make sure the grass under your feet looks good and feels great.

Autumn Essentials

The summer is coming to an end, the temperatures are dropping, and the evenings are losing their light. Your lawn is still very much in play, but needs to be managed slightly differently, so it can ride out the winter as strong and healthy as possible.

OVERSEED

The grass plant takes a lot of stress through the winter so you want to make sure the lawn is as dense as possible with fresh, new growth while you can. Get an overseed down now (see pages 76–80 for more information) while the temperatures are still high enough for strong germination and rainfall is up again. You'll be thankful the following spring!

AERATE

Get ahead of the game for a wet winter and aerate the lawn before all the rainfall comes in the colder months. With a little moisture now back in the lawn after summer, aeration will be effective and also help to remove the compaction from all those summer games on the grass. (See pages 64–71 for how to aerate the lawn.)

SCARIFY

As the weather remains hot, you'll want to remove any debris sitting on your lawn, which may end up suffocating your grass. Use a rake (or a scarifier) to clear your lawn of any debris. (Read our scarification section on pages 58–63 for more information.)

CUT BACK ON THE MOWING

Mow the lawn as and when required. If you've going back to once a week or once a fortnight, you can still double-cut each time to get a higher quality of presentation, and reduce the stress on the grass plants.

Winter Essentials

Winter has come around again and the main priority is to stay inside and keep warm. The days of dancing behind your lawn mower in shorts and T-shirt are long gone. You miss it, we understand. However, this doesn't mean there isn't anything to be done to make sure your lawn comes out fighting in the spring.

KEEP FEEDING WITH A WINTER FORMULATION

Feeding all year is crucial to a strong, healthy lawn. Winters are very testing time for plant survival, so making sure we feed and give the grass that extra help in fighting disease is really important. This also maintains a good base for the transition to spring. There is no playing catch-up and trying to recover the damage created by the winter – it's straight into presentation mode. This is also when our plan tackles moss with a small amount of iron in the feeds (see page 84 for more).

REMOVE ALL LEAVES, DEBRIS, AND TOYS

There's nothing worse than the grass plant being smothered in the winter when it's already fighting hard to survive, it doesn't need the extra pressure. Whip round with a rake and remove all those soggy leaves and children's toys that are just going to kill off the grass underneath. We certainly don't want to score any own goals and create more repair work.

CUT ONCE A MONTH

It is still okay to cut the lawn once a month at this time of year if it's required and to keep things looking tidy. It's more likely that the mower has had its last outing (although not guaranteed), so after a long hard year at work now would be a great time to give the mower a good clean, especially inside the deck where clippings will have gathered.

BOOK YOUR MOWER IN FOR A WINTER SERVICE

Don't wait until spring to get your mower ready. While it isn't getting much action at the moment, now is a good time to get it booked in for a service. The blades should be sharpened so they are ready to put a good shift in next year; getting the mower serviced when you need it twice a week can be quite a pain.

STAY OFF THE FROST

Frosty mornings are coming! When the lawn is frozen it's best for the plant if it doesn't get a lot of foot traffic as the leaf is extremely brittle. Needless to say, there is definitely no need to get the lawn mower out.

AERATE

Winter is a great time to aerate your lawn as the wet ground is easier to penetrate. This is useful as over the winter your lawn will become cold, wet, and compacted, so the roots can't access the nutrients. (See pages 64-71 for more on aeration.)

Glossary

Aeration The process of perforating the soil with small holes to allow air, water, and nutrients to penetrate the grass roots.

Annual weeds Weeds that complete their life cycle in one year and typically spread through seeds.

Annuals Plants that complete their life cycle in one growing season, from germination to seed production.

Biennials Plants that require two growing seasons to complete their life cycle, typically vegetative growth in the first year and flowering in the second.

Broadleaved weeds Non-grassy plants with wide leaves that commonly invade lawns, such as dandelions and clover.

Compaction The compression of soil particles that reduces pore space, hindering root growth and water infiltration.

Core The cylindrical plug of soil removed during aeration to reduce compaction and improve airflow and water absorption.

Cool-season grasses Grass species that perform best in cooler climates, with active growth during spring and fall.

Crown The part of a grass plant where the roots and shoots meet, crucial for new growth.

Cultivar A specific variety of a plant that has been selectively bred for desirable traits, such as drought resistance or fine texture.

Dethatching The mechanical removal of thatch build-up to allow air, water, and nutrients to reach the soil.

Dormancy A period when grass growth slows or stops, usually due to unfavourable weather conditions.

Fertilizer burn Damage to grass caused by over-application of fertilizer, leading to browning and potential plant death.

Frost heave The upwards or outwards movement of the ground surface (or objects on, or in, ground) caused by the formation of ice in soil.

Fungicide A chemical compound used to prevent or eliminate fungal diseases.

Glyphosate A non-selective herbicide used to kill all vegetation, often used for total lawn renovation.

Herbicide A chemical substance used to control or eliminate unwanted plants (weeds).

Integrated Pest Management (IPM) A holistic approach to pest control that combines cultural, biological, and chemical methods to minimize environmental impact.

Imbibition A phase during germination when the grass seed absorbs water.

Irrigation The artificial application of water to the lawn to supplement natural rainfall.

Leaching The downward movement of dissolved nutrients or chemicals through the soil, potentially leading to groundwater contamination.

Macronutrients Essential nutrients required by plants in large amounts, including nitrogen (N), phosphorus (P) and potassium (K).

Micronutrients Nutrients required by plants in smaller amounts, such as iron, manganese and zinc.

Mowing height The recommended height at which to cut grass, varying by species and seasonal conditions.

Mulch A layer of material applied to the soil surface to conserve moisture, suppress weeds, and improve soil health.

Mycorrhizae Beneficial fungi that form symbiotic relationships with plant roots, enhancing nutrient and water uptake.

Nitrogen (N) A key nutrient that promotes lush, green growth in lawns.

NPK The three primary macronutrients in fertilizers: nitrogen (N), phosphorus (P) and potassium (K).

Non-selective herbicide A herbicide that kills all vegetation it contacts, used for total vegetation control.

Overseeding The practice of spreading grass seed over an existing lawn to improve its density and health.

Perennial weeds Weeds that live for more than two years, often with deep root systems making them difficult to eradicate.

Perennials Plants that live for more than two years, often with deep root systems, returning each growing season.

pH adjustment The process of altering soil pH to optimize conditions for grass growth.

pH level A measure of the acidity or alkalinity of the soil, which affects nutrient availability for grass.

Phosphorus (P) A nutrient that supports root development and overall plant health.

Photosynthesis The process by which green plants use sunlight to synthesize nutrients from carbon dioxide and water.

Post-emergent herbicide A herbicide used to kill existing weeds after they have emerged.

Potassium (K) A nutrient that aids in disease resistance and drought tolerance in grass.

Pre-emergent herbicide A herbicide applied to prevent weed seeds from germinating.

Radicle The part of the embryo of the grass plant seed that develops into a root to anchor the seed in the soil.

Rhizome An underground stem that produces roots and shoots, allowing certain grass species to spread.

Rootzone A specialist soil preparation.

Root zone The layer of soil where grass roots grow and interact with nutrients, water, and microorganisms.

Scalping Cutting the grass too short, which can stress the lawn and lead to weed invasion.

Scarification The process of removing thatch and moss from the lawn's surface to promote healthy grass growth.

Seed mix A mixture of seeds of different grass species or cultivars combined to achieve desired lawn characteristics.

Selective herbicide A herbicide formulated to target specific weed species without harming the desired grass.

Soil amendment Materials added to soil to improve its physical properties and nutrient content.

Soil test An analysis conducted to determine soil nutrient levels and pH, guiding fertilization and amendment practices.

Stolon A horizontal, above-ground stem that takes root at various points, aiding in the spread of some grass types.

Sward A dense, continuous expanse of grass covering the ground, forming the visible lawn surface.

Thatch A layer of dead grass, roots, and debris that accumulates between the soil and the green grass blades.

Tiller A sideshoot that grows from the base of a grass plant, contributing to lawn density and recovery from damage.

Top-dressing Applying a thin layer of soil or compost over the lawn to enhance soil quality and promote grass growth.

Transpiration The process by which moisture is carried through plants from roots to leaves, where it changes to vapour and is released into the atmosphere.

Turf/sod Pre-grown grass and soil held together by roots, transplanted to establish a new lawn quickly.

Warm-season grasses Grass species that thrive in warmer climates and grow actively during the summer months.

Index

Pavilion
An imprint of HarperCollins*Publishers* Ltd
1 London Bridge Street
London SE1 9GF

www.harpercollins.co.uk

HarperCollins*Publishers*
Macken House
39/40 Mayor Street Upper,
Dublin 1
D01 C9W8
Ireland

10 9 8 7 6 5 4 3 2 1

First published in Great Britain by Pavilion
An imprint of HarperCollins*Publishers* 2026

Copyright © Pavilion 2026
Text © Luke Taylor and Marc Kerr 2026

Luke Taylor and Marc Kerr assert the moral
right to be identified as the authors of this work.
A catalogue record of this book is available from
the British Library.

ISBN 9780008756031

Publishing Director: Laura Russell
Editor: Shamar Gunning
Copyeditor: Katie Hewett
Editorial Assistant: Daisy Gudmunsen
Designer: Lily Wilson
Layout Designer: maru studio G.K.
Production Controller: Grace O'Byrne
Illustrator: Sarah Abbott
Proofreader: Annelise Evans
Indexer: Vanessa Bird

Printed in Malaysia by Papercraft

The author and publishers do not accept any
responsibility for any injury or adverse effects
that may arise from the use or misuse of the
information in this book. Be careful when
handling chemicals.

WHEN USING MACHINERY PLEASE
ALWAYS FOLLOW THE MANUFACTURER'S
INSTRUCTIONS.

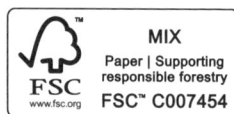

MIX
Paper | Supporting
responsible forestry
FSC
www.fsc.org
FSC™ C007454

For more information visit:
www.harpercollins.co.uk/green